COOKING
FOR COMPANY
How to Do It With Ease & Elegance

by
Hedy Giusti-Lanham

BARRON'S

WOODBURY, NEW YORK • LONDON • TORONTO • SYDNEY

Credits:

Photography:
    Matthew Klein, color photographs
    Susan Johnson, stylist
    Andrea Swenson, food preparation

    credits for accessories given on page 273

Jacket and cover design: Milton Glaser, Inc.

Book design: Milton Glaser, Inc.

All inquiries should be addressed to:
Barron's Educational Series, Inc.
113 Crossways Park Drive
Woodbury, New York 11797

Library of Congress Catalog Card No. 82-11410
International Standard Book No. 0-8120-2699-3

Library of Congress Cataloging in Publication Data
Giusti-Lanham, Hedy.
   Cooking for company.
   Includes index.
   1. Entertaining.   2. Cookery.   I. Title.
TX731.G54   1983   642'.4   82-11410
ISBN 0-8120-2699-3

PRINTED IN THE UNITED STATES OF AMERICA

3 4 5 6   880   9 8 7 6 5 4 3 2

CONTENTS

For all the great hosts and hostesses,
from New York to San Francisco,
and from Minneapolis to Dallas,
who bravely overcome all kinds of difficulties
and give splendid parties.

PREFACE

People have been entertaining since ancient times.

As the idea of "social obligations" probably didn't exist at the time of the Pharaohs or the Roman Consuls, they must have thrown those banquets because they enjoyed doing it. Granted, they didn't have today's problems of lack of space or lack of servants, but they must have had other difficulties. How did hosts in ancient Rome cope with the draught in their marble palaces, with the female guests wearing nothing but flimsy togas? And what did they do about refrigeration on a hot Egyptian summer day?

Ages have different problems. This book shows you how to cope with the ones most of us have today.

There are different reasons for entertaining. First, there are people who *must* entertain: diplomats for whom it is part of the job, or international industrialists who have to make important contacts in an atmosphere that is more relaxed than their offices. Also, businessmen who travel and are entertained abroad know that it's their turn when their business partners come to this country.

Second, there are people who *feel* that they have to entertain. "You are only as good as your last dinner party," said one hostess to me recently. "If you want to be in the swim, you have to entertain constantly or people will forget you." (I suggest that the lady get herself a new set of friends who won't forget her if a month goes by without an invitation. Also, you wonder if she feels the same. Does she drop people who don't invite her constantly? Where does she find the time for all those parties?)

Finally, there are the people who *love* to entertain. This book is really for them.

The diplomats don't need this book. They usually have houses or very large apartments; they have servants; and they have an entertainment allowance. Their wives train to be good hostesses from the beginning of their husbands' careers and, by the time they come to this country, they are so good at it that nothing throws them.

It can, of course, happen that the allowance runs out when they have a particularly heavy period of visiting VIPs. I remember going with the wife of a diplomat to pick up some special pizza and smuggle it into the service entrance of the embassy. It made a rather inexpensive party and no one noticed.

In the case of industrialists and other businessmen, it depends what rung of the success ladder he or she has reached. If the host or hostess is at the top or near it, space, help, and money probably present no problems. But for those who are only just getting there, often there are problems. What does the wife of a young and ambitious businessman do if her husband travels to countries where ten servants are still considered a way of life? She is okay until her husband's business associates come to this country and have to be entertained. They can be taken to a restaurant, but it's not quite the same thing. Also, a dinner for, say, six people might easily cost as much as the husband has just made on the deal with his guest.

If you, like me, have to entertain foreigners for lunch, take them to your club (or to the club of a friend where such arrangements can be made). Most clubs have buffet luncheons, which eliminate the need to make decisions. I have had disastrous experiences with foreigners who are not used to our way of ordering. "Crabmeat? Ah, yes. I would love to try it...just a small portion. Then I think I will have beef, done whatever way you recommend. American beef is so much better than ours. But not too much, mind you. Yes, a small salad. Cheese? Yes, but only a soupçon—no lunch is complete without the taste of cheese. That's all, thank you. Unless I could have a little more wine. Just half a glass, thank you."

What that person didn't realize is that we don't have half a glass of wine and a "small portion" of crabmeat. A glass of wine is a glass of wine, and a soupçon of cheese is a cheese course. By taking them to a club you can avoid all this. (The club might, of course, declare bankruptcy.)

But for dinner, alas, there are very few buffets. According to what problem (money? space? help?) you face, the following chapters might solve it.

The people I am really talking to are those who love to entertain—for the sheer pleasure of it. And the people who are not quite sure. And the people who are terrified of it.

You can be a great cook and not have a lot of money or a lot of space. Quite! But I doubt that a truly great cook would hesitate to entertain just because he or she doesn't have a dining room. His or her parties would be the talk of the town just because of the splendid food. And the host would know it and feel totally secure, even with plastic forks and almost no table decoration.

The recipes in this book do not include those spectacular gourmet dishes which usually require a lot of time, frequently a lot of money, and always a lot of knowledge. Instead these recipes are simple. Most of them originate in my native Italy or were created by Italians living abroad. The important point is: serve unusual food, as simple to prepare as your everyday fare, and present it with a flair. You'll overcome your problem, whatever it is.

Great cooks are immortal and a legend in their own time. This book is for mortals.

PREPARING FOR
THE PARTY

I t's Tuesday afternoon, and you've just hung up the phone at the office and you are facing the prospect of giving a party. A feeling of panic starts to come over you as you wonder how you'll decide what to serve, when you'll get the marketing done, and if everyone will be able to eat what you prepare. Pre-party jitters are common, so don't think you're the only person who worries about whether it will all go right.

Entertaining people in your home can and *ought* to be fun, both for you and for your guests. And making your cocktail or dinner parties, picnics, or after-theater gatherings successful is usually more a matter of planning ahead and using your resources than having any talent or special ability. Your food can be simple, your decorations minimal, yet the event will be outstanding and memorable for your friends if you set aside a little time now. Here are a few basic "musts" that will help you organize your thoughts and get you moving.

THE RAW INGREDIENTS

Have a complete marketing list, down to the last lemon. Keep your list flexible, meaning that if you plan to have stuffed artichokes as your first course, fine. But if you go to the market and you see artichokes that are gray and tired, don't buy them just because you had planned to serve them. And don't get rattled either; have an alternative ready. Stuffed zucchini? A spinach mold? It should be something you have made many times before and feel good about. (Never try something new for a party.)

Do your marketing well in advance; last-minute shopping can be a disaster. Get everything except highly perishable items such as berries. Even parsley, if you place it in a canvas bag—one of the best inventions of recent years—will keep beautifully fresh.

In the days before the party you may have to clean out your refrigerator to make room for your party ingredients. Feed your family cheese sandwiches to use up extra bread and cheese. Don't buy that roast for dinner this week; you know you won't have the space for leftovers.

In spite of all your precautions you may still not have enough space for your party food, especially if you are planning a very big affair. If you live in the country, you will probably be able to park some things with a neighbor. If you are in an apartment building in the city, you should know at least one other tenant moderately well; you might ask that person to extend hospitality to some of your groceries. (Best not to ask them to hold a fish for you, however.) And make sure to tell your neighbor that you would be happy to do the same for him or her another time.

If you can't ask a neighbor for help, remember that our mothers didn't always have refrigerators and they coped. Do you have a cool room in your house? Bread, fruit, cheese, even eggs and butter usually don't have to be refrigerated. They survive happily in a cool, ventilated room overnight or for a few hours before the party. If your party is to be in the summer, however, you'll have to be more careful about what you choose to store for any length of time without refrigeration. Dairy products, for example, shouldn't be left out in warm weather.

KEEPING FOODS HOT OR COLD

Just before the party there might be a few appetizers that need to be chilled, yet the refrigerator is already stuffed with other food. Try to chill things in shifts. Supposing you have a plate of stuffed eggs and a bowl of raw vegetables. Unless they are chilled, the former get soggy, the latter get limp. Place the vegetables in the refrigerator first, and when they are really crisp, take them out and put a few ice cubes in the bowl; the vegetables will stay crisp for quite a while. In their place in the refrigerator put the eggs, until you are ready to serve both.

Whether you serve it in drinks or use it to keep your food cold, you can never have too much ice. If you have your own ice maker, you have no problem. But how many of us have one of those? And no matter how many trays your freezer produces, it will never make enough ice cubes for a large party. So you should plan on buying ice—plenty of it.

If you have an old-fashioned Skotch Kooler, you will find that it will hold quite a lot of ice for a long time. Unfortunately, these coolers are no longer available, and the fancier ice buckets don't hold as much ice and don't keep it as long either.

The answer is to place the ice in a huge metal tub, and put your wine bottles into it. Such a relief for your refrigerator! And you can also put the butter on the ice, as long as you keep it in a plastic container.

If you think you have no space for such a metal tub, think again! Place it in your bathtub. People won't see it, and if they do, they will admire your inventiveness.

If you do use the tub as a means for chilling foods, be certain that everything you place in the ice is tightly closed. The first time I used that method I got carried away. I was so pleased with my wonderful idea that I took a bowl of chicken salad out of the refrigerator and placed it among the ice cubes. It sat there, perfectly balanced and safe, until the ice started to melt. My chicken salad did not survive the break-up. Fortunately the party was a buffet, and there was plenty of other food. The chicken salad would really have been redundant...or so I told myself.

Keeping foods hot is a different matter, and no neighbor or ice bucket can help you. I keep reading recipes that tell you to "remove the chicken breasts (or shrimp, or veal cutlets) from the skillet and keep warm." They don't tell you how, especially when you are making enough to serve eight or ten people.

One way is, of course, to keep the just-cooked foods in the oven. Turn off the heat and wait until the oven is comfortably warm, then place the foods in. But I find that, whereas the foods will stay warm okay, they will also dry out. A stew will survive, if well covered, because it has a lot of liquid, but sautéed meat or fowl will resent this treatment.

The solution is a hot tray. Or more than one hot tray. I own three, in various sizes, and I am just waiting for the next sale in a housewares department to buy yet another. With few exceptions, foods will stay nicely warm—even very hot—on such a tray until you are ready to serve them. Get the ones that have an adjustment for heat level.

FLOWERS

I discuss flowers in several of the following chapters, but there is one problem to mention here: how to keep them fresh if you don't buy (or pick) them at the last moment.

Not all flowers require the same treatment, but a couple of rules go for most. Place an aspirin or two (depending upon the size of the vase) in the water. Change the water every day and, if at all possible, cover the blossoms very loosely with newspaper overnight.

No matter what you do, don't resort to plastic flowers! They are the only thing worse than no flowers at all. Branches of green leaves are preferable if flowers are impossible or, if you really must use artificial flowers, purchase some pretty silk ones. They are quite expensive, but they last.

There are people who feel unsure about arranging flowers. This subject could take a whole chapter if not a whole book, and could consider the various types of flower arrangements that are possible. Personally, I am not very fond of Japanese flower arrangements, with their strict rules about height of the stem in relation to width of the bowl. But if you are good at it, go ahead; it certainly is a striking way of presenting flowers. I prefer a more informal or spontaneous arrangement. A large bunch of baby's breath is lovely even by itself. Add a few peonies or carnations and it becomes spectacular. Sometimes the spontaneous arrangements are so successful I have taken pictures of them. I remember one grouping of baby's breath with white lilies; I have never been prouder of my living room.

Stay away from iris, beautiful though they are, because they don't last past one day and they also drip nectar. At today's prices it isn't easy to replenish flowers frequently, but do have them when you entertain.

SETTING THE TIME

One very important point for a smooth-running dinner party is knowing at what time you want to sit down for dinner. Your time is approximate, of course, but even if you have a cook in the kitchen, you should know when you want to eat.

Supposing you have invited people for 7:30. Do you want to eat at 8:30 or at 9? If the dinner is on a weekday evening and people have to get up early the next day, I would opt for 8:30. But the hour is not what matters. Just pick the time and stick to it.

Allow all your guests to be a half-hour late and then serve those who have arrived. An exception to this rule would be a weather-related incident such as a sudden blizzard, in which case you are lucky if the guests get there at all. In situations such as these guests are forgiven, and you are excused if your food is past its prime.

I find that people are usually polite, and they realize their being more or less on time is important. I have, however, said more than once to a late guest, "you have time for one quick drink; dinner is ready." No one minds. And that is much preferable to seeing the other guests (the early ones) have another couple of drinks they don't need, or catching them looking at their watches while they listen to their stomachs growl.

I remember a party that should have been an informal pleasure but turned into a formal disaster. The hostess was the tense type, that evening particularly because the guest of honor was a famous writer who had a wife who was a famous hostess. To compete with her would have been folly, so we planned a very simple menu, counting on the wit and charm of the congenial group she had invited. Unfortunately, one not-so-congenial couple chose to be two hours late.

We had drinks on the terrace, which was beautiful in the sunset, but the weather turned cold and dark an hour later. In spite of my desperate signals, the hostess just didn't have the courage to serve dinner without the two missing guests. (They too were rather famous.) When they finally arrived it was quite obvious that they had had a fight. Her eyes were red and she sniffled quite a bit; he looked grim. They obviously needed a drink, and the hostess, in her mercy, allowed them to have one. Then dinner was served. It was food, but overcooked to the point of being difficult to recognize. I heard the guest of honor mumble, "And for this we have waited two hours?"

SETTING THE DATE

The only thing that is worse than guests arriving very late is for them not to show up at all.

Be careful how you invite and when you invite. Meeting someone on the street and saying, "Would you come for dinner a week from Thursday?" is very dangerous. They might accept—without their calendar in front of them to check whether they have another engagement, or to write down the one they have just made with you.

The best method is to confirm by phone. You can also send a

reminder, but when will it arrive? There you are, counting on your guests, and a day before your party they call to say that, terribly sorry, but they had just gotten your note and looked up next Thursday. Oh, dear... They feel badly, and your party is just not quite as you planned it. You might be able to fix it if there is someone you know well enough to invite at the last minute, saying, "Please come if you can! You would save my party."

It is also not a good idea to invite people by mail, with the request *R.S.V.P.* noted at the bottom. Some people take their time before replying, and then you wait, not knowing how many people are coming. That method is alright if you invite way ahead of time or if you are planning such a gigantic party that a few people more or less won't matter. Short of that, you should know well in advance how many people are coming.

In summary, the best way to invite is to ask people by phone, when they have their engagement calendar in front of them and can give you an immediate reply. Then send them a reminder or, if that is too formal, call them again a few days before your party. This method should be foolproof.

For me, it has been foolproof, except for one bachelor friend. I once invited him—casually—to a cocktail party and he didn't show up. My fault: I had given him a chance to forget it. Next time I asked him—quite formally—to a buffet supper honoring a guest from abroad. He accepted with pleasure and asked if he could bring a friend. (He too had a guest from abroad.) Sure, his friend would be welcome. Neither of them showed up, and not a word of explanation! I ran into him some time later and asked him where he had been that day. "In the Caribbean," he said not a bit embarrassed.

He will find himself somewhat short on invitations, I think. I know of at least four people who have taken him off their list. The trouble is that he is so completely innocent, at least in his own eyes. He is a poet who lives in a dream world and forgets about us poor mortals. He should say, "I would love to come, if I can remember" and whoever invites him takes his or her chances. But he is definitely an exception. Most people show up, more or less on time, provided you invite them properly.

In recent years a new type of invitation has been added which, frankly, I find rude. The invitation, elegant or not, gives you all the pertinent data and adds under the R.S.V.P. "Regrets only." This makes it quite obvious that the party will be a mass production. As a friend of mine says, "I don't regret; I don't reply and I don't go." I am not quite that drastic—I regret, but I never, never go.

INVITATIONS AND PLACECARDS

Don't get cute. There are many ways to show that you are an imaginative person, but party invitations, if you are sending them, should be clear and simple.

Funny faces and cut-outs from the comics are great for children's parties, but for adults a white card (or some solid colors), either handwritten or printed with the necessary information, is the only elegant way to invite. For some special holiday, such as Christmas or New Year's, a red card with black letters is a nice change. But garbled invitations that are supposed to be cute are as embarrassing as babytalk from an adult. Whenever I get an invitation that is elaborately "amusing" I feel inclined to answer in the negative.

The same rule applies for placecards; white cards with a silver or gold edge (or just plain white) with the name of the guest clearly written in your best handwriting. If the party is for a baby shower or a birthday, you could use a light blue or a pale pink, but—please— no funny drawings instead of a name. These antics have your guests guessing who is supposed to sit where while the soup gets cold.

MARKING THE WAY

If you live in the country or in the suburbs, check that your driveway is well lit. If there is a name of the street where you live, be certain the sign is visible, as well as the number of your house. If this can't be done, have your name on the mailbox and a light nearby. And if you expect several cars, make sure the guests can see where they should park.

Your entrance will, of course, be brightly lit. If you have a doorbell or knocker, ascertain that they are loud enough for you to hear late-comers, even if the early guests are very noisy. I found myself one winter night at the door of a brightly lit house, with music streaming out of every pore, knocking until my arm was tired. I finally ran around to the back of the house and came in the kitchen entrance; the cook heard me.

On another occasion a host had gone to the opposite extreme. The party was in a beautiful villa in the French countryside, far from the nearest town. To be certain his guests would find the way, and also to set a festive mood, he placed torches on both sides of the country road for about half a mile. We found the villa, alright. The trouble was, so did everybody else. It seemed that the whole of France had been invited, and when the time came to leave, we found our car blocked by a dozen other cars. There was no one to move them, and no keys left in the cars. I got back to my hotel about 5:30 in the morning, too tired to remember how spectacular the buffet had been.

If you live in the city, these problems don't exist. But whether you are in a townhouse or an apartment, make sure you can hear the doorbell or buzzer.

And then there is one small but important touch. If there is a mirror in the elevator, no problem. If not, hang a mirror on the wall just outside your door. There is no guest who does not want to take one last look before making an entrance.

AMENITIES

I don't serve cigarettes any longer, in the hope that people won't smoke. You do, however, have to have ashtrays around because people bring their own cigarettes. The ashtrays should not only be plentiful, they should also be large. Those cute little things that hold only one butt won't do if you have a party of more than two people. And they have to be emptied all the time.

Actually, emptying the ashtrays goes for large ones as well. Stale tobacco smell doesn't go well with food. And speaking of odors, it is best to stay away from serving cauliflower or Brussels sprouts. If you can't live without them, cook them well in advance and then open the window or turn on the fan. You can reheat them quickly when you are ready to serve dinner.

For just general cooking odors, there are some marvelous perfumed candles around. They cost a fortune and are great if you get them as a gift. There are also some cheaper ones, but the scent is less acceptable. Another device, much less known than the candles, are little felt rings sold together with a small bottle of the essence of a flower. You drop a few drops of the essence on the felt ring and place it around the base of a lightbulb. When you turn the light on, the heat of the bulb will bring out the perfume. An easier way is to take an eyedropper and place a few drops of your own perfume on a couple of lightbulbs before you turn on the light.

Let's not forget the bathroom. You have taken care of the guest soaps and towels, but have you overlooked the garments hanging on the back of the door? No matter how pretty your nightgown and no matter how elegant your husband's robe, they are your private business.

I feel similarly about the towels and soap. When you have guests, only their towels and their soap should be visible in the bathroom. Hide your own towels, even if they are wet from a pre-party shower or bath. I have been known to put mine in a plastic bag and hide them under a pillow.

GETTING READY

This is really a point meant more for the lady of the house. Of course you want to look your best. Just as you like to show off your lovely china and most beautiful crystal, you want to show yourself off as well. There are two things to keep in mind, however: don't overdress and don't be uncomfortable.

Unless you are absolutely certain that your guests will arrive in the same type of attire, don't wear an evening gown. It is better to underdress than overdress. And a simple hostess gown is fine, but you must consider if you will be comfortable and able to move about. This is how I once made a mistake. I wore a straight, simple dinner dress with a rather tight skirt. There are only five steps between my dining room and kitchen, but they seemed a major obstacle as I tried to travel back and forth, carrying platters or bowls and holding up my skirt to manage the steps. Everyone had a good laugh at my awkwardness, but since then, when I know that I will have to move about a lot, I wear pants. They are a marvelous solution, provided they are straight-cut. Wide-legged silk pants can get you in as much trouble as a full skirt.

Men hardly need to be told what to wear. Chances are they will wear pants (unless they wear kilts), so it boils down to "tie or no tie." In the city, it's obviously "tie" and in the country probably "no tie." If there is the need for any special attire, the host will certainly advise.

SOME SPECIAL
SITUATIONS

NO TIME

This is a problem that confronts me often—not daily, but so frequently that it seems daily. I can't resist the temptation to ask people for dinner, for supper, for Sunday lunch, or for after the theater. It never occurs to me to ask myself where I will be an hour before they arrive.

If all goes well, I get home from work around 6 P.M., or a little after. If I have asked people for 7:30, the timing is not too bad. If I have asked them for 7, I am in a jam. And I usually ask them for 7.

People who work (and who doesn't nowadays?) like to get home at a reasonable hour, whatever that is. If you allow an hour or so for drinks and appetizers, you start dinner at 8 or shortly thereafter. By 10:30, people begin to go home.

Let's say you have asked people for dinner for 7, and you get home at 6. Don't trust the old belief that people are never on time; when you least expect it, the doorbell rings at 7 sharp. Make sure you are not in the tub. Or, if you are, that there is someone to welcome the guest and to say, "Mary (or Lilly or Jane) will be out in a second. In the meantime, may I fix you a drink?"

But no matter how skillful that person is at making excuses, it doesn't look good. It makes the guests feel that they have been too prompt. The answer is: be ready!

BEGIN EARLY

How do you manage to be ready in time for your guests? First, set your table ahead of time. Not just the evening before; you need that time to prepare your food, or at least part of it.

I have been known to set the table a week before the party. I cover it very lightly with tissue paper to avoid even a speck of dust on the plates or glasses, and I remove the paper very carefully when I am ready to place the candles in their holders and to put the butter and bread on the table.

Appetizers are very time consuming to prepare, particularly if you insist on little sandwiches. I find that they have seen better days, and don't care if I never see another. Usually the bread is a little soggy by the time it gets passed around, and who needs all that bread before a good dinner anyway? And yet tiny sandwiches are back in fashion even at the grandest parties—such as a recent splendid affair at the Metropolitan Museum of New York—probably because people are tired of cold quiche.

If you like a large bowl of crudités (raw vegetables), that are so "in" with people for whom overweight is so "out," you can cut radishes into rosettes and celery into strips the night before. Place them in the bowl in which you intend to serve them and fill the bowl with water. Place the bowl in the refrigerator and, when you are ready to serve the crudités, just pour off the water; they will be crisp. After you fix the vegetables, prepare a dip (if desired), cover, and refrigerate.

Stay away from sliced zucchini and cauliflower rosettes. The former get tired looking if they are soaked for too long and the latter tend to turn brown. But do try sliced raw fennel. Many people are not familiar with fennel, and yet it is such a marvelous vegetable, both raw and cooked. Just be certain you buy the male variety and not the female. The male looks like a round, fat bulb, whereas the female seems as if it has been flattened from both sides. The fennel may be sliced also the night before, but little cherry tomatoes need nothing but rinsing just prior to serving.

Cheese platters are a problem. You can't readily prepare them ahead of time because they will smell up your kitchen, if not your whole apartment. If you keep the cheeses in the refrigerator and only take them out as soon as you get home, they will still be too cold when you are ready to serve. (Cheese should always be served at room temperature.)

There are two basic cheeses you can serve without problems: swiss and provolone. Cut either, or both, into small chunks, then put them in a bowl, cover it tightly with wax paper, and place the bowl in the refrigerator the night before your party. Remove the bowl in the morning before you leave the house; at dinner time it will be at the right temperature and the cheese will not have smelled up the apartment nor run. In the evening you need only toothpicks for people to help themselves.

A BUFFET TABLE

One way of serving that makes sense when you are short on time is a cold buffet. And a great, though expensive, main course is a cold fish. When I say "cold," I really mean at room temperature. A poached striped bass or salmon, served with a good homemade mayonnaise or a tartar sauce, is a spectacular dish.

Poach the fish the night before and let it cool in its own cooking liquid (water with a couple of stalks of celery, a small onion, and a teaspoon of peppercorns). Remove the fish to the platter on which you intend to serve it, slip off the skin, and pour a little of the liquid over and around it. Cover the platter with wax paper and, if you can possibly do so, allow the fish to cool slowly (not in the refrigerator). Put it on a windowsill, if you have one. Turn off all the radiators and let your family freeze for a day—anything rather than put the fish into the refrigerator. When the time comes to serve it, the fish will be at room temperature, with a nice little gelatin around it. Decorate the fish with a few sprigs of parsley and some lemon wedges (you could cut up the lemon the night before as well and wrap it in wax paper).

Serve a green bean salad to accompany the fish. If beans are not in season or they look wrinkled in the store, frozen ones will do. Or, if you are lucky enough to live near an oriental grocer, buy some long beans. They are marvelous for the salad; just cut them to the desired length before you boil them.

Prepare the beans the night before, then refrigerate them overnight, but remove them from the refrigerator as soon as you get home the next day. Toss them with a little vinegar and a lot of good olive oil. If you wish (and if you have the time), sprinkle some very finely chopped parsley over the beans.

You can wash and dry the greens for the salad the night ahead also, especially if you have a canvas bag to keep them fresh. Even so, I suggest you look at the greens carefully when the time comes the next day to place them in the salad bowl. There might be some little browning on the edges, particularly if you use greens such as Belgian endive or bibb lettuce, which are more fragile.

My system for a delicious salad is to place the dressing in the bowl, mix it very well so that the oil, vinegar, and mustard, if any, are perfectly amalgamated. Then add the greens and toss vigorously.

AT THE LAST MINUTE

As this dinner is planned, the guests will nibble on crudités and cheese with drinks, then proceed to a cold buffet table set with poached fish, green bean salad, tossed salad, and later dessert. If you review the timetable, your last-minute preparations are something like this:

1. Remove crudités and dip from refrigerator and uncover the cheese. Toss the salad. (2 minutes)
2. Decorate the fish. (5 minutes)
3. Toss the green beans and then pour the mayonnaise into a bowl. (5 minutes)
4. Arrange the flowers, both on the table and wherever else you wish them. (10 to 15 minutes)

You have time left to bathe and dress for your party, and be ready for your guests when they arrive.

WHEN THE GUESTS ARRIVE

Just before the doorbell rings, place pats of butter in two or three places on your buffet table. When the appetizers have been eaten and the apéritifs drunk, place the bread in the oven. Toss the salad greens in the dressing and place the salad bowl on the table. Remove the bread from the oven and put it into a basket. Cover with a napkin and place it on the table. Now call your guests to the table and enjoy the food.

This is an ideal situation: except for the bread, all the food is served cold. If someone dawdles, you need not get frantic. The fish will be the most decorative thing you can grace your table with, especially with a sauce dish of glorious mayonnaise on one side and the green bean salad on the other.

The guests will help themselves, but you will need someone to stand by the fish and watch it. The reason for this is that there comes the moment when the top half of the fish has been removed and the spine stares you in the face. There has to be someone who knows how to remove it and will do it quickly. Otherwise you will have one of your guests, totally unfamiliar with that particular fish, try to turn it over to get to the other side. The result will be a fish hash without any distinction.

I have a little trick I find priceless. Before I poach the fish, I open it wih one hand and, with the other hand and the help of a very sharp knife or pair of strong kitchen shears, I cut the spine just under the head. When the time comes to remove the bone, it lifts off without the slightest trouble. Of course if you can afford to have a person serve the meal, he or she will remove the spine and make it disappear into the kitchen without any fuss at all.

ALTERNATIVES

The meal described is an easy dinner, not time consuming at all. it is also quite glamorous, but it certainly isn't cheap. The fish should be large enough for two helpings per guest. If you have leftovers, you will have a great fish salad the next day, but a fish of impressive dimensions is very, very expensive. And there is also the matter of whether your guests will want to eat fish; not everyone does.

If you are unsure and don't want to chance it, there is another version of this no-time dinner; it is also a lot cheaper, but it is less elegant: a baked ham or a special meat loaf.

If you opt for the ham—either whole or half a ham—remove the fat on top, baste the ham with red wine, and if possible, leave out the customary pineapple. The important thing is that you bake it the night before the party, let it cool, and slice it. When you have cut off all you think you will need, place the slices back against the uncut part of the ham and, after every ten slices or so, secure them with toothpicks until the ham looks as if it hadn't been cut. Cover it with wax paper and refrigerate it if you must. (Better if you only keep it in a cool place.) On the evening of the party all you do is remove the toothpicks and voila! (If you wait until the last moment to cut the ham, you will spend half an hour slicing. By putting it all together again, you will prevent it from drying out.) I often use a ham from West Virginia, a "semi-boned." Very satisfactory!

This meal is no problem, no great expense, and you can feed your family for a week on all sorts of marvelous concoctions based on left-over ham or meat loaf (p. 213). But whichever you choose, stick with the green bean salad. Make a huge bowl of it; there is something puny about a small salad and, if you have some left over, it is delicious the next day. If served with fish, add a little mustard to the salad dressing; with the ham, omit the mustard. Ham tends to be salty, no matter how you bake it. Lastly, if you want a truly impressive buffet you can serve both a fish and a ham. It is great for the company, but not for your finances.

One would think that you could prepare a whole roast beef the night before and serve it cold the next day. You can, but not very successfully. If you slice it just before your party it will take a long time, particularly if you are pressed for time and therefore a little jittery. If you slice it the night before, it will look like deli food by the time you are ready to serve it.

There are all sorts of casseroles that may be prepared the night before and baked just before serving, but I find that they present some danger. If you have placed them in the oven for thirty minutes and are having a good time with your guests, you might forget them and the result could be disastrous. Set a timer and make sure you can hear it over conversation that is bound to be lively.

Desserts are no problem. Practically any baked dessert may be prepared the night before or even two days ahead. If you don't care much for serving sweets, cut up fruit into a large bowl and allow it to marinate in its own juices for twenty-four hours. At most, you can add a little liqueur at the last moment: rum, brandy, or—if you prefer a sweeter taste—Grand Marnier or Amaretto. The choice is endless.

And, finally, I always have some good lemon sherbet in my freezer, not only for my no-time dinners, but also for my unexpected guests. I scoop the sherbet into individual bowls and pour a little Poire or Framboise liqueur over. If I want to be extravagant, and have a few more minutes, I pulverize a few *amaretti* (hard Italian macaroons) and sprinkle them over; it looks good and tastes heavenly. Both Poire and Framboise liqueurs are expensive, but a bottle lasts a long time, unless you develop too much of a taste for the liqueur.

Whichever version of these no-time dinners you choose, marketing can be done the day before and in less than one hour. The only item that might present a problem is the fish, particularly if you are not an experienced fish buyer.

If you have a reliable fish market, trust them and hope for the best. If you want to be personally responsible for your fish, the first rule is to smell it; it should smell of the sea and not of stale heating oil. It used to be said that underneath the gills should be bright red, but this is no longer a guarantee; some fish markets use red dye on them. The critical thing is the eye. If it is covered with a gray film, the fish has seen better days. And if you don't mind touching the raw fish, there is yet another test. Poke it with your finger; a fresh fish is elastic, not stiff.

AFTER THE THEATER

To invite people for after the theater (or a concert, for example) is a reckless thing to do unless you have someone to help you. (Ideally, that "someone" should not have also been to see the show, but should have been in the kitchen preparing things.) However, I have given after-theater parties without any help and have also had a lot of fun doing it.

You can make such a party quite lovely, with tables set up for, say, six or eight persons. Stay away from a long buffet table at that time of night; somehow it doesn't seem to work with a group of people discussing the merits of the performance and the lack of cabs after, or—particularly—wanting to use the bathroom. The group is restless, and you must account for this.

Before leaving the house, arrange the bottles and glasses on whatever surface you have: a sideboard, a table, an improvised table set up in the entrance, or even a table in the kitchen. The important thing is that they should be within reach. Have plenty of ice and be sure the glasses are in plain view. If you wait until you get home before you open the liquor cabinet and get out the glasses, your party is out of control.

Also have something within reach to munch: simple things like pretzels, potato or corn chips, little cheese-flavored crackers or imported olives. Let the guests fix their own drinks while you disappear into the kitchen, but make sure you have plenty of paper napkins.

Somehow, on a cold winter night after a show, onion soup is a must (page 144). No one expects a full meal at that time of night. And, if you need to feed your guests standing up or sitting down wherever they choose or wherever they find a spot, you could serve soup in mugs. No need for spoons or saucers; it makes life a lot easier.

On your tables could be cold meats, with two or three interesting mustards and dark bread that you had buttered before you went to the show. People can make their own sandwiches or eat the meats as they choose. By all means make a salad. The greens could be washed before the show, the salad dressed when you return. Have two large carafes of wine—one white, one red—and refill them when people look thirsty.

All of this can be followed by a plate of cookies, possibly homemade. Be sure you have a lot of coffee on hand, both full strength and decaffeinated. If you want to have another alternative, serve some herbal teas.

SUNDAY LUNCH

I don't know why I associate Sunday entertaining more with the country than the city. Maybe it is because there are so many Sunday afternoon events to go to in the city. But in either place, a Sunday lunch is a lovely institution for both host or hostess and guests. And if your weekdays are short on time, Sunday entertaining may be your simple solution.

Your Sunday party will be most successful if you have it at a time other than during a football or baseball season. During these times, the sports fans usually cluster around the television and the others are left out. But, assuming there are no ball games to distract, your guests could nicely number about a dozen. If you don't go to church you can do most of the preparation in the two hours before your guests arrive. If you do go, you can prepare most everything the evening before, then get up a little earlier on Sunday to complete the rest of the preparations before leaving for church.

For the liquid part of the menu, prepare two pitchers: one with bloody Marys (the Lord will forgive you) and one with bullshot, unless you know exactly what your friends drink (in which case you can prepare accordingly). Have plenty of chilled white wine as well; I find that two out of three people ask for white wine nowadays.

Unless it is bitter cold, you are unlikely to serve anything hot. If you feel that your guests will need to be defrosted, you might want to give them a cup of hot consommé to begin. The cups and saucers are an extra bother, though, requiring additional clean-up as well. Again, use mugs.

Place everything on your buffet table ahead of time. If it is around the holidays, avoid ham and turkey because people will have been getting their fill of it from November through January. Instead, a special chicken salad is a marvelous dish (page 191). And then there is the almost infinite variety of rice salads (pages 185–187). Platters of chicken salad and rice salad are complemented nicely by a platter of raw vegetables and, possibly, a cheese platter.

Dessert? Do your guests really want anything more than cookies or brownies? I doubt that people will want a rich dessert, especially if they are going to have supper later. If you do wish to serve dessert, make it very light. (See the pear mousse, page 253).

These dishes may all be prepared the night before, and, even then, they take only a little time to put together. Whatever your situation, you can offer your guests a lovely time and an excellent dinner or luncheon without making the meal a hassle for yourself.

Buckwheat Noodles with Olive Sauce, page 168

NO MONEY

H aving no money is a malady that seems to be reaching epidemic proportions. Speaking about money used to be considered bad taste. One either had money or one didn't, but it was never acceptable conversation. Nowadays dinner conversations are sprinkled with prices of filet of beef, extra-large eggs, and Parmesan cheese. The high cost of entertaining is the obvious reason.

For someone such as I, who would sacrifice taking cabs—or even taking buses for that matter—rather than give up having guests, money problems are a challenge. "No money" certainly means no professional help, which is the most expensive item about entertaining, but it can also mean carefully considering what foods and drinks you serve and how you present your home. You might be lucky enough to have talented and willing family members to help you prepare, serve, and clean up, but coping with the rest of the problems is your job.

DECORATIONS

"Flowers are too expensive," someone said to me recently, "I use artificial flowers." I find artificial flowers utterly depressing, even the "almost real" type. As I mentioned in an earlier chapter, however, nice green leaves can be charming and lush; it all depends on how you arrange them. If you have the space, fill a very tall vase with long branches and place it on the floor in a corner. It will look dramatic, particularly if the leaves are glossy.

One has to be a little careful, though, if picking the greens oneself. A European friend had recently come to this country. She loves to go on long walks in the country. It was in the fall and she saw some beautiful red leaves, unlike any she had ever seen before. She was going to have some people in for a small dinner in her tiny apartment and thought how good the leaves would look. She picked an armful, and had to call off the dinner. It was poison oak. I don't recognize poison ivy or oak, but I stay away from anything with three shiny leaves.

And leaves aren't always needed. I often like to have a low center-piece on the table because it gives the table a focus. It can be a small bowl with one flower in it, or a pretty porcelain figure or animal. Or, if you have the space, try a large bowl with fruit in it that will then be eaten at the end of the meal. If your budget is tight, however, you can assemble a lovely centerpiece from what you have or can acquire for very little money.

I once had some large glass beads, for which I had no further use. Then came a dinner party. It was the middle of winter and flowers were outrageously expensive. I placed a large, clean cauliflower in the center of the table. (I had removed all the leaves and cut the stem somewhat so that it would stand flat. I placed a piece of paper underneath that didn't show but which would protect the table-cloth.) Then I stuck the multicolored beads into the cauliflower with toothpicks. And I cooked the cauliflower for dinner the next night.

Glass beads are available in Japanese stores for almost nothing and can also be used over and over. But you could also use paper but-terflies. Just make your arrangement simple and striking, and don't use so many props that the cover the cauliflower completely.

All sorts of vegetables lend themselves to table decorations. Pep-pers, particularly if you mix red, yellow, and green, look festive and gay. They are difficult to place on the table, however, unless you buy a quantity and pile them into a large bowl. If you want to invest in just a few, use one of the newer pronged gadgets for baking potatoes. Place one pepper on each spike, leaving them on various levels. Then add another three peppers, leaning them against the spiked ones. You might add a few radishes to hide the empty spots.

Long candles are expensive and can also be a nuisance, but you do want the glow of a flame at your table, since it makes everyone look very attractive and lends a festive air. Get those little votive candles instead. They don't cost much and the containers can be used forever, simply by inserting a refill (which cost very little as well). And they have an additional advantage: if you have a backyard or a deck where you like to entertain during the warm season, you can use citronella candles in them instead.

Beware of one thing when you select candles: make sure they aren't scented. I was at a dinner party not long ago given by a hostess a bit too imaginative. She wanted multicolored candles, not realizing that each would have a different perfume. It was difficult to eat in this cacophony of scents. Too much perfume, even the best, can ruin anyone's appetite, but bad perfume and several kinds mixed can be ruinous.

You will probably want to use your prettiest dishes, but don't worry that they don't match. Or rather, if you are eight for dinner, the eight dinner plates should match but the salad plates (if any) and the dessert plates needn't match the dinner plates. In other words, you don't need a set. In fact, using different plates shows more imagination.

The same goes for glasses. I have inherited some very pretty wine glasses. I suppose they were once a set, but that was long ago. Now three or four match, and the rest are an assortment. I get more compliments for them than I would for a perfectly matched set, no matter how beautiful. And as for flatware, if you don't have silver, don't fret. Stainless steel is perfectly acceptable. And not only is there some pretty stainless around, but the knives and forks really don't have to match either. No one looks to see if his or her neighbor has a fork that looks exactly like his own. And if there are people who pay attention to such details, don't invite them.

SERVING DISHES

Even the simplest of food can be presented elegantly. Suppose you decided to serve a platter of raw vegetables; I can hear some people say, "to present all those vegetables elegantly, I'll need a large silver platter and I don't have one."

Those large silver platters belong on the late, late show. And porcelain, whereas it can be beautiful, also is easily broken. But wood is handsome and durable, as long as you serve the vegetables without seasoning. (Wooden bowls and platters absorb the odors and oils of garlic, onion, oil, and so forth. They become sticky and eventually turn rancid.) There are some very pretty bamboo trays on the market. They are not expensive, but they don't last too long.

I have a passion for lacquer trays. Of course nothing is more beautiful than an old lacquer tray from the Orient, either red or black, but the modern Japanese trays are also charming and quite affordable. They also last a long time, provided you don't cut on them; they scratch rather easily.

Lucite also scratches easily, but such trays are easy to find in the stores and are very durable. But any black tray—lacquer or Lucite—will look marvelous holding multicolored vegetables, with just enough space between the rows for the black background to show through. It beats any old-fashioned silver tray.

Nor do you need precious platters for most meat dishes. If a stew was cooked in a casserole it can come to the table in its original dish. Only a roast—beef or veal—and a whole fish have to be transferred to a platter.

There are some very attractive and inexpensive earthenware platters in most houseware stores. Chances are that your roast costs as much as they do, but if you plan to entertain frequently and serve a lot of roasts, you might consider purchasing one.

Lastly, I own a few glass salad bowls which originally came with flowers from the florist. I use them frequently for salads. Or, if you receive flowers in a wicker basket, when the flowers fade, wipe it clean, place a napkin in the basket, and use it for bread and rolls.

THE FOOD

When considering the cost of entertaining, your immediate thoughts are probably of the food. if you are not careful, appetizers can cost a fortune. Besides, those heavy old-style canapés ruin people's appetites and, unless you serve something truly spectacular, no one will remember the appetizer anyway. And we do want a little credit and admiration for our efforts, don't we?

A large platter of raw vegetables, mentioned as a solution to other problems as well, is always good to eat and pretty to look at. Make your platter look lush. I went to a cocktail party recently and found only about twenty strips of celery in a little bowl. How depressing!

Make sure that you buy only what is in season; hothouse vegetables are expensive. Peel some medium-sized turnips and slice them. (There is a gadget that makes perfect rounds and costs very little.) You could also slice carrots. Arrange the slices in a row, each round slightly overlapping the previous one. Then make a row of green— zucchini, cucumber, for instance—and follow with more carrots, this time cut into strips. Then celery, also in strips (if cut into strips, the celery outer stalks are also useable, provided they are not too fibrous.) If broccoli is not too expensive, make a border of little flowerets all around.

You might feel that your guests can't survive on vegetables alone. Get a small mozzarella—made from whole or skim milk—and a package of small pita breads; see the recipe for Pita and Mozzarella Canapés (page 134).

If you wish, add a large bowl of corn chips to your selection. People just pretend that they are kid's stuff; they love them, particularly the foreigners. (I should know; I am one of them.)

Someone mentioned to me recently that she planned to use paper plates and paper napkins at her dinner parties. "There are some charming ones around... and they are cheap." This is partly true: charming they are; cheap they are not.

Just plain old-fashioned paper plates, the kind you buy in a supermarket, are neither pretty nor practical. They will be done in by sauces and gravies, and once they get flabby they are not attractive, nor are they appetizing. There are also the new glossy plates, very pretty and even gravy-resistant. But after dinner you have to throw them out.

I have figured out that four sets of paper plates would pay for one set of plain porcelain or earthenware which would last a long time. The same is true of paper napkins. They are fine for cocktails when you use a lot of them, but for dinner, cloth napkins are cheaper, even if you have to wash them.

Sometimes the problems of "no money" and "no help" overlap. This is certainly the case with your tablecloths. How do I feel about permanent press cloths as opposed to linen? I don't like them, but I do use permanent press, for two reasons.

Hand me an iron and an ironing board and I am lost! I either get the iron too hot and burn everything, or I keep it too cool and don't get the wrinkles out. On the other hand, I learned my lesson one time when I got carried away and used a spectacular tablecloth I had owned but had never used. It was long enough for twenty-four people, but I used it at a table for sixteen. it was greatly admired and then went to the laundry the next day. Of course it came back looking marvelous, rolled over a cardboard contraption, but the bill from the laundry was just a little more than the cost of the entire meal.

If you have a beautiful dinner table with a glossy, immaculate surface, you don't need a tablecloth at all. Nothing is more attractive than beautiful wood. The most you might want to use are placemats, though if they are linen, they are just as much trouble as a cloth. Straw placemats often are quite lovely and plastic ones frequently are not. Sometimes just a small Lucite disc is sufficient to protect your table.

If your dinner table doubles as a work table for the kids, or if you use a card table that you set up for dinner, the "no cloth" solution is no solution at all; use an attractive cloth.

How about the dinner itself? Have your grocery bills been so discouraging lately that the idea of buying food for eight or ten people depresses you? Remember that we are all in the same boat and the boat is a little leaky.

No one really expects smoked salmon as their first course, with a filet of beef to follow anymore. All your guests want is something good to eat, served with a little imagination. The best solution is to turn to ethnic foods, especially those of the Chinese and Italians. They have been cooking on a shoestring for centuries.

I knew nothing about Chinese cooking, but a little while ago I decided to invest in a wok. I still know very little about this varied and resourceful cuisine, but what I do know I enjoy greatly. I started by asking the Chinese merchant from whom I bought the wok all sorts of questions, and from him I learned how to stir-fry and steam vegetables. Then I bought a little book on Chinese cooking and began to improvise and adapt. I discovered bean curd (tofu) and started using it in all sorts of ways, not all Chinese. The one thing to keep in mind about tofu is that it is highly perishable. Buy it only in a natural foods store where it is kept under refrigeration; it should be pure white, not yellowish. When you prepare tofu, cook it for at least two minutes, a little longer if possible.

The one drawback I found to this type of cooking is the matter of storing the wok. If you have a small kitchen or are short on space, you won't know where to keep your wok when not using it. And if your stove is electric, you need to have an attachment.

I've known about Italian cooking since I started entertaining at the age of seventeen. Italian cuisine is neither heavy nor greasy, and in recent years people all over have become much better acquainted with its many facets. It is not all veal (expensive), fish (also expensive), chicken, and pasta with tomato sauce.

There are pasta dishes that are light and yet can easily constitute an entire meal. And in spite of the astronomic price of Parmesan cheese, most pasta dishes are still inexpensive. If you have a chafing dish and wish a dramatic touch, try *La Spadellata* (page 166).

And not only are there elegant pasta dishes, there are also rice recipes that you can make as expensive or inexpensive as you choose. Lastly, there is an almost infinite variety of vegetable dishes also.

There are many foods that are inexpensive and delicious, but which some people don't like. I am thinking particularly of items such as chicken livers or kidneys. One either loves them or hates them, so if you want to serve such things, make sure first that your guests like them. There is nothing worse than having a guest try to eat something he or she obviously can't enjoy and then finally having to admit that fact.

Chicken livers are among the cheapest meats on the market and even if you prepare them with mushrooms, they won't bankrupt you. Kidneys are in the same category, but make sure you know how to prepare them nicely (page 227).

The ideal background for these meats is rice, but if this combination strikes you as too banal for company, try two other cereals that are equally good and a lot more unusual: barley or buckwheat.

Barley is one of the cheapest foods on the grocery shelf, and it is very easy to prepare. Just follow the package instructions and boil it for ten minutes less than they say. As for buckwheat, get the whole kernel variety (usually sold in natural foods stores); the buckwheat in most supermarkets becomes a mush when cooked. I still like it, but as a breakfast cereal, not a side dish for meats. Use half the amount of water they tell you on the package, and taste the groats after 3 minutes; they might be done.

Some of the hefty soups (see pages 142–144) are inexpensive, unusual, and enjoyable meals for your dinner guests. But if you think you can buy them in a can instead of giving them tender care by simmering them for several hours, think again. Canned soups are a poor substitute for the homemade variety. Besides, they are more expensive than soups you can make in your own kitchen.

If you feel that a pasta dish or rich soup—no matter how good—is too informal for the dinner you have in mind, how about a beef stew? (see page 215). Or try a veal stew (page 226). The latter will be more expensive because the veal for the stew has to be good, which means that it isn't cheap. If you feel that the word *stew* isn't elegant enough, give it a fancy name, possibly in a foreign language.

Most people think that no meal is complete without a salad. And, generally speaking, I do too unless your main dish features lots of Chinese vegetables or is a sturdy Italian vegetable soup. But when salad is to be served, you'll have to count on spending a large part of your budget on good greens. Different types of lettuce have become expensive items in the store, unless you use iceberg lettuce, which I don't recommend. Bear in mind when you shop that salad leftovers cannot be reused, so buy only as much as you need for your party.

Leftover salad brings to mind a dinner party (I was a guest, not the hostess) where the first course was a horrible tasting soup, served in very fancy lacquer bowls. The hostess, knowing my interest in food, asked me coyly if I cared to guess what it was made of. I assured her that I couldn't possibly. (I had a hard enough time trying to eat it.) She said, almost triumphantly, that it was made of leftovers of various salads, puréed and heated!

Now for your dessert. The word itself conjures up visions of complicated, gorgeous confections that are hard to make at home and very expensive to buy ready made.

It used to be that cheese and fruit was an inexpensive and unusual dessert, but although it still can be unusual, it certainly isn't cheap. Fruit, when in season, is still affordable but cheeses have reached prices that are impossible. (I sometimes feel that it would be cheaper to let the mice eat up the house in the country rather than buy cheese to set traps.)

There are, however, some delightful desserts that cost very little (see pages 249–269). And I find that people love them just as much as those fancy concoctions based on expensive chocolate and imported liqueurs. Lastly, it seems that those big desserts have become a thing of the past now that everyone is so calorie- or cholesterol-conscious.

All anyone really wants after a satisfying meal is a taste of something sweet. It is what the French call *bonne bouche:* something that will take the taste of meat or fish out of your mouth.

WINE

Unless you have some really fine palates among your guests, it is perfectly acceptable to chill a couple of two-liter bottles of wine. These larger bottles are much cheaper and easier to chill than the equivalent amount of wine in regular bottles. There are some excellent jug wines on the market, particularly the white wines. Most of them are Italian, although the California wines are good too but usually a little more expensive.

If you serve wine with your appetizers, then continue if you can with the same wine for dinner, but decant it. There is no need for a precious decanter, however. There are plenty of glass decanters available that are actually one-half or one-liter bottles, and some florists use them as vases.

Place one bottle or decanter at each end of the table (or have one white and one red, but bear in mind that the white wine will disappear first). Even the least experienced wine pourer will be able to manage the decanters.

AFTER DINNER

One doesn't see these trays of liqueur bottles, with golden, amber, or green liquids, anymore. Some hosts or hostesses will still ask you if you would like an after-dinner brandy. That's all, and even that is something you shouldn't feel obligated to offer. You should, however, have a tray of water glasses, particularly if you have served Chinese food that has been laced with soy sauce.

Serve coffee, however; that is still a must. And remember that it should be good coffee, freshly brewed. Decaffeinated coffee can be brewed now too, and it is the ultimate courtesy to offer that to your guests.

I prefer to prepare my coffee using a filter system. There are several methods of making filtered coffee, depending upon the manufacturer, and they are all good. Percolated coffee is not as good because you have to watch it. If it percolates too long, it gets bitter;

if it doesn't percolate long enough, it's thin and undrinkable. I also feel that a filter brings out the best in coffee.

I like to serve after-dinner mints. Forget the ones that come in fancy boxes; you don't eat the box and you probably won't even serve them out of the box. There are perfectly good mints in supermarkets which come in little bags. They taste of mint, which is all mints should do.

NO SPACE

T his can be a nuisance, but it is a problem that can be dealt with if you organize whatever space you have.

Let's assume the worst: you have a tiny kitchen and no dining room. Your kitchen is narrow and not very long. The narrow part gives you an advantage: you can stand in the middle and reach both the sink and the stove, as well as the counter on the other side. Think of the poor people who have a gigantic kitchen and wear themselves out running from one end to the other!

KITCHEN MATTERS

Obviously you have some cabinets for china, glasses, and maybe silver. Between the cabinets and the sink underneath there might be some space. That's where you could hang a shelf that would run the whole length of the wall; it is where you could keep your spices and condiments. Maybe you can even put up two shelves, one above the other; the second shelf could be where you store everyday glasses. (You'll have to keep your good glasses enclosed somewhere else, lest they get dusty.) If the shelves are to be long, they won't be a standard size, so have them made. Surely you know someone who has a saw and would be willing to cut boards for you. If not, get two long boards cut at a lumber yard and paint them yourself with a hard enamel or varnish to make them waterproof. The people at the lumberyard will also give you suggestions on how to attach the shelves to your wall. Make sure they are firmly secured.

Whatever bare wall space you have can be covered with pegboard. I am a one-woman disaster area with a hammer and nails, but even I can handle pegboard. It is very easy to install and is relatively inexpensive. You'll need to buy both the pegboard sheets and wooden strips to place between the wall and the pegboard.

Once you have it installed, hang all your kitchen utensils on the pegboard, particularly the ones you use most. And here comes a very important point: use small utensils, geared to a small kitchen. You don't need a gigantic colander because you won't be feeding twenty-four people. A smaller one will do and it won't take up as much space on your pegboard. You also don't need a huge wire whisk; a smaller one does the trick and is easier to handle. Get a plastic measuring cup. If you knock it off the wall, it won't break. Hang a couple of small saucepans on the wall: to melt butter, to boil an egg.

When you are ready to cook, think of all the things you will need and have them near you. It isn't so easy to move around in a small kitchen, but you can do a lot to make it all easier when you are under pressure.

Take, for example, a time you are going to make a white sauce. The refrigerator is probably within easy reach from where you stand at the stove. Or maybe you have a half-size refrigerator under the sink. Take out the butter and start it melting over a low flame; put the rest back in the refrigerator. Get out the milk and, as soon as you have used what you need, put it back too. Don't clutter up the space with things you don't need.

Have your wire whisk within reach, as well as the nutmeg, salt, and pepper. And have the other foods you will be cooking either assembled together on your counter or in the forward part of your refrigerator. In any event, your refrigerator should be well organized. If you are preparing for a party, don't fill it with things you won't need for another three days. And have those items you need for your party within easy reach.

Choose your menus with space (the lack of it, that is) in mind. Make appetizers that stay in the refrigerator until the last moment, and main courses that perhaps are one-dish recipes which can stay in the oven until serving time and that won't take up counter space. If you keep your preparations simple and the ingredients and tools organized, you should have no problem working in even the tiniest of kitchens.

I once knew a woman who had complained to me about her kitchen. "If you saw it you would know why I can't entertain." I went to see it. It was small, all right. And there—over the stove—hung a wooden sign saying "God bless our mortgaged home." Without the sign, there would have been space for a rack of knives and spoons. The spice shelf in her kitchen held a few little bottles of artificial everything, including a few porcelain dogs. (She called them "doggies.") When I suggested that she could perhaps do without them— or the sign—she said that in such a bad kitchen she needed something to cheer her up. It depressed me. But she belongs to that tiny group of people for whom it is probably better to take guests to a restaurant, if she can manage without her "doggies" for an evening.

Assuming that you would really like to have friends for dinner and would prefer a functional kitchen to a cute one, you might still wonder where you could keep your platters and bowls. Presumably, there is no more room in your tiny kitchen.

One time my husband and I were visiting relatives in Texas. They have a ranch, and the outdoor space is unlimited but the indoors is rather skimpy. Other relatives from all over the state were coming to see us. Unexpectedly, the parents of our hosts called to tell of a change in plans: they were not coming by car, but instead were flying in and needed to be picked up at the Dallas airport. Our hostess was a bit upset, since it would take two hours to get them at the airport and bring them back to the ranch. Whereas the cook was perfectly able to cope with the food, she was not capable of presenting it elegantly. I offered to help, and, as she had one leg in the car, the anxious hostess suddenly turned and came rushing back. "The platters are under the sofa in the living room," she shouted in my direction. Sure enough: platters of all sizes, bowls, even a lazy Susan.

And why not? Everything was neatly covered with plastic and ready to use. The space under the sofa was just high enough to hold the platters and not high enough for the kids to crawl into. Think about it: don't you have some unconventional storage space?

DINING ARRANGEMENTS

Is your problem that you don't have a dining room? Do you have a part of the living room that can be used for dining? Let's assume that you do.

Don't worry that a table set up for dining is in full view. A pretty table (and you are, of course, setting a pretty table) is not only inoffensive, it actually adds a festive touch. But maybe you don't have enough space to set up the table and still entertain guests for cocktails. Then perhaps you have a drop-leaf table you can open when the moment comes to eat. Drape the tablecloth over it and place the plates and flatware on the narrowest part of the table. You'll have everything handy. When you want to open the table, lift first one leaf and set up the plates, then raise the other leaf. Presto! No need to remove all the plates.

You also need bread. You probably don't have enough space on the table for bread and butter plates, and they are unnecessary. Serve breadsticks instead of rolls or bread. Breadsticks don't require butter (butter is baked in) or butter plates.

Obviously it might not appeal to you to have the breadsticks roll all over the table, nor should they. I have thin silver rings, somewhat like wedding bands for a great Dane, and they hold about five thin breadsticks or two to three thicker, seeded ones. I inherited them, but you could use those pretty straw napkin rings sold in all Japanese stores and in some five and dime stores. They come in lovely colors, and they hold breadsticks beautifully. Choose ones that fit your dinnerware and place them on the left in front of the plates. If there is no space, place them on top of the napkins, which in turn are placed on top of the plates. Your guests will remove them when they sit down, but until then they look charming.

There was a time when you had to have two wine glasses and one water glass for each guest. No longer! Water shortage or not, no one expects a glass of water by his or her plate. (If someone wants water, he or she asks for it.) And with the white wine craze, you don't have to bother with two wines. Your guests will drink white and enjoy it with any meal, unless you are serving steak or venison; somehow it seems impossible to serve white wine with either.

Another trick is to use luncheon plates and salad forks instead of full-sized ones. No one notices, and they take up much less space. And then there are the candles. We all love them, and maybe you have a pair of beautiful candelabra on your mantle. But how will they fit on your crowded table? They won't; don't even try. Light them where they are, and they will add a gentle glow to the room. And for your dinner table, use small votive candles, scattered wherever you have an empty inch.

CLEANING UP

Dinner is over and you move into another corner of the room for coffee or after-dinner drinks. You will do the clean-up later, after the guests have left. Be adamant about this, no matter how they pretend to want to help you. Nothing is worse than several bodies trying to operate in a kitchen that can barely house one.

But what about the table?

A prettily set table is one thing; a table full of dirty dishes is quite another matter. So hide it behind a screen!

We would all love to own an antique Chinese lacquer screen but not many of us do. Buy a skeleton of a screen in an unpainted furniture shop and cover it yourself. I am a disaster with anything but kitchen utensils, but I needed a screen for my office to hide a sink and a small refrigerator. I bought one of those wooden frames and a young student of design covered it for me with posters. It looks charming and cost very little. You might not want posters for your screen, so use wallpaper. When the screen isn't hiding anything it stands demurely against the wall and makes a pretty decoration.

Let me add another small warning: if you have anything strongly scented left on the table, remove it to the kitchen quickly, without commenting on it. I once went to a dinner in a small apartment. Everything was lovely and the meal ended with fruit and cheese. It was perfect, except that one of the cheeses was a very strong one. It was not removed to the kitchen and, although the table was hidden, waves of camembert floated over the after-dinner conversation. Not so good!

WITH EVEN LESS SPACE

Suppose your living room is not big enough to act as your dining room. Do you have a small entrance hall where you can set up a folding table *after* the guests have arrived? I have lived with one of those arrangements and found it quite satisfactory; it's just a question of organization.

If you have to open drawers and cabinets to find flatware and plates, you will make a mess of your party. If the hostess leaves her guests for too long, they feel ill at ease. And if the guests hear cupboards opening and closing, they feel guilty. (The poor woman is working so hard.) But if you have everything prepared in one place where you can easily find it, you can call upon one person to help you set up the table, and then you can set it yourself in a jiffy. You go back to your guests smiling.

You have no place to hide all the dinnerware? The kitchen is too small, and you can't use the space under the sofa because your guests are sitting on it. The bedroom is no good because the guests have put their coats on your bed. (Besides, maybe you have no bedroom and the sofa becomes your bed when the guests have departed.) Ah, but you do have a bathroom! Guests usually don't use the bathroom at the beginning of a party, so you place a board across the tub and put all your things on it: plates, glasses, flatware, salt, and pepper—everything! It will take you three minutes to set the table.

You don't have an entrance hall big enough to hold even your umbrella? Do you have space for a set of small folding tables? When not in use they remain under the sofa or even under your bed. When they are needed, set them up wherever your guests are sitting before you serve dinner. Then they can get up and help themselves from a sideboard or even from the kitchen. Or you can do the serving; it will avoid the confusion of people standing around with full plates in their hands, not knowing where to sit down (or, worst of all, trying to behave nonchalantly by sitting on the floor, making it impossible to move around them or for anyone to serve the wine.) If you have ever coaxed someone with a full plate on his lap to get up from the floor, you know what I mean.

And now comes the last resort: you have no space to set up small folding tables and your guests will have to balance the plates on their laps. This used to be difficult even before so many people in this country started drinking wine; now it's practically impossible. How do you balance both a full plate and a full glass?

Where there is a problem there is usually also a solution if you only look for it. Recently some very pretty trays have come on the market, just large enough to hold a plate, a glass, and a piece of bread. They can be of plastic (in pretty solid colors or—as I prefer—colorless), or of raffia, or even of heavy coated paper. And you can store them anywhere when not in use.

Don't try to pass the butter around once the guests are seated with their trays. They can't spread it on the bread anyway, unless they have three hands. Serve small buttered rolls or some sort of breadstick that needs no butter. Very trendy!

Another warning: don't serve a course with a lot of gravy or sauce. Some of it is bound to spill onto the tray and you would have to remove it, together with the plate. If the tray had remained clean, you could replace the dinner plate with the dessert, and the wine glass with the after-dinner coffee. Then also, no one spills anything in his or her lap or on your best rug.

SOME SMALL SUCCESS STORIES

I know a hostess whose gift for entertaining is hard to match or to copy, but I'll tell you about her anyway. She lives alone in a charming apartment with a dining room that seats six if no one gets up; she also has a tiny, but very well organized kitchen. She has a job, but loves to have guests for lunch. Granted, she lives close to her place of work, but when she says "We will eat at one" you may be sure that you will sit down at one. She has two great assets: her personality and glorious porcelain and silver. An invitation to her luncheons is a treat.

The day I am thinking of we sat down to a table set with beautiful plates, each one holding a gigantic boiled artichoke, with a little bowl of delicious sauce next to it. In the center of the table stood a large bowl of museum-quality porcelain. In front of each plate we had a little finger bowl with warm water. As we ate our artichoke, we placed our leaves in the bowl in the center.

The conversation was witty, helped along by our hostess, who was obviously enjoying herself too. When the bowl was full, our plates empty, and our fingers rinsed, she stretched out her left leg, opening the swinging door to the kitchen and, with one rapid movement of her hand, emptied the bowl into the garbage can which was just two feet from her. Then she reached for another bowl, this one of a delicious crabmeat salad that had been on a sideboard behind her, and passed it around. We kept the same plates and emptied the bottle of white wine that was on the table in its lovely wine cooler. (No wine is served with artichokes; they destroy your palate.) Then we moved to the living room, where she served coffee and brownies. Shortly after two o'clock she was back at work.

She would clean the table in the evening and probably prepare it for another luncheon the next day. Everything was done with such ease and enjoyment. Had she seemed harassed or worried, no porcelain, no matter how precious, would have saved the party.

There is another thing to remember: if something goes wrong don't let on! Whatever happens, try to fix it without anyone noticing.

If someone breaks a wine glass and you don't have a spare, use your toothbrush glass and pretend it is your favorite and you *always* drink wine out of it. Never, never say "Good heaven! It was the last one, and they have stopped making this pattern!" If you do, you will see a curtain of gloom descend on your party that no one will be able to lift.

This very thing happened to me once. A guest dropped an ice cube into a glass so thin that it was almost invisible. It cracked. I said to the maid, "Remove that glass, please, or Mr. —— might cut himself." Would that he had—to shreds! It was indeed an irreplaceable glass but, had you seen me smile, you would never have guessed. No one's mood was ruined except mine.

But this is not the only reason why I mention this incident. Disasters can happen when you have all the space you need and all the help you want, but they happen more frequently in cramped quarters. It is easier for someone to drop a glass of red wine on your white rug if he has to balance that glass on his knees. If this happens, pour a bottle of soda water over the spot and blot it up with paper towels. (This has to be done right away before the wine dries.) Your guests will understand; but don't let it get you down.

In conclusion, let me tell you another story. The other day a charming young woman approached me with a problem. She had found the almost-perfect apartment. The rent was affordable and for the first time since she left home she wouldn't have to share it with anyone. It had a view; it had thick walls which meant that she wouldn't hear her neighbors sneeze; and it was within walking distance to her office. She was happy, but the kitchen had a two-burner stove and half a refrigerator.

"It's fine for me alone, but how can I ever have guests? I have space in the living room to set up a table for four, but how can I cook a meal on a two-burner and so little refrigerator space?"

Just the kind of challenge I like. "You will make the kind of minestrone that is practically a meal-in-itself" (see page 218). "You will start it the night before, and turn it off just before you go to bed. Then you will continue to simmer it in the morning and, keeping the heat as low as it will go, you can even keep it going all day. If you are working that day, and are afraid to leave it on, you could turn the stove on again as soon as you get home. That will give you two more hours at least. It's not perfect, but it will do. When I get there I will make the second course, though you don't really need it. Anyway, all the stove I need is one burner, and all the food I need is one carton of eggs and a stick of butter. As dessert, I would suggest some sherbet. If you take the ice trays out as soon as you get home from work, you will have the space for the sherbet."

I told her exactly what to buy for the minestrone and how to go about making it. The next evening I grated some Parmesan cheese at my house and brought it to her as a house-warming present. She seemed flushed and thrilled with her preparations.

I proceeded with the preparations for the Basic Frittata (page 164), which I was going to fry after her guests had arrived. It turned out to be almost too much. After a minestrone like the one I taught her, no one had much space left. Anyway, I wanted her to see what could be done with two burners.

There was no need for a salad; minestrone is so full of vegetables that even one leaf would have seemed redundant. There was also no need for cheese with all that Parmesan in the minestrone and on top of the frittata. And, once I had removed the frittata from the stove, she had both burners to make coffee: one more than she needed!

Someone had sent her a bottle of Crème de Menthe for her new apartment. We poured it liberally over the lemon sherbet. Even without the liqueur, it would have been a most successful evening.

NO HELP

T he most common complaint when entertaining is discussed is "I have no help." It is a remark that is becoming contagious, and there is no relief in sight. There are three forms of it: no help in the kitchen, meaning there is no one to do the cooking; no help in the dining room, meaning there is no one to serve the food; or—worst of all—there is no help at all.

"No help" can mean that you have no access to hired help, whether it be a cook or a maid, but it can also imply that there is no husband, wife, or friend to help you prepare the food, serve it to your guests, or clean up afterwards. Regardless of the circumstances, if we can assume that the person involved would like to entertain and is not using the "no help" as an excuse, there are ways to overcome such obstacles.

NO HELP IN THE KITCHEN

Let's assume the worst: you have no help at all, or what there is is so inadequate that you might be better off without it. If money is no problem, there are caterers, and some of them are excellent indeed.

Caterers come in all categories, from those who prepare the food; deliver it complete with maid or butler; supply plates, flatware, and tablecloths; then take it all away again to those who cook the meal for you to pick up and take home, allowing you to serve it as you wish. Between these two categories are dozens of others, of various nationalities and talents. The one thing they all seem to have in common is the price: they are all high.

In addition to the caterers is a totally new industry, which I call ready-to-wear food. These are shops that sell freshly prepared dishes for you to reheat or not, and which look and taste so home-made that you can serve them without losing your dignity, particularly if you add your own appetizers and side dishes.

I remember my first experience with this kind of arrangement. Some years ago I knew a charming hostess in a lovely brownstone in New York City. Her husband was an architect and he had built her a perfect kitchen, but he forgot to build her the perfect cook. At that time there was no ready-to-wear food industry to speak of. The hostess had a responsible job but, whereas she appreciated good food, she had little talent or interest for preparing it. She also didn't have much time. She did prepare great appetizers—beautifully displayed—and her table was among the most exquisite I have ever seen. And her guests were always fascinating.

We would sit in the living room, which was also the dining room and occupied the whole ground floor, having a drink and some appetizers until the doorbell rang. She would answer it, on the run, while instructing us to sit at the dinner table, quickly! We could see the door from where we sat; there was a panting lad who had obviously been running. He handed her a large, flat package which she opened, placed on a platter, and served immediately.

She had gotten friendly with the owner of a pub in the neighborhood. He had one specialty: beef and kidney pie, and we were eating it. The pie was superb. If anyone had told that pub owner that he was perhaps New York's first caterer, he would have wondered what the word meant. He simply liked the lady and knew that she couldn't cook.

If you need just a little help, you don't have to go looking for a pub. It can be a friend who is particularly good with one dish and would prepare it for you and not tell. (Yes, you also invite her for dinner.)

Or your source of food might be a restaurant where they know you well or a club to which you belong. The important thing in this situation is to solve the problem of the main course. Surely you can add your own salad, your own vegetable or other side dish, and your own appetizers.

A woman once complained to me that entertaining had become so frightfully expensive, what with having to hire a cook every time she had a few people for dinner.

"If only I could cook a little dinner myself. Nothing elaborate, you understand...."

I assured her that she could. I started describing an unusual vegetable that can be prepared ahead of time.

"Get five medium-sized zucchini and grate them coarsely."

She interrupted me. "And ruin my manicure?" Actually she wouldn't ruin it at all. Zucchini are soft and grate easily. And she wouldn't have to grate them to the very end. But she wouldn't hear of it.

"Okay, forget the zucchini. Bring a lot of water to a boil in a large pot..."

"And let the steam ruin my hairdo?" She was quite angry and, at this point, so was I. I suggested that she take her guests to a restaurant and we never touched the subject again.

Sure, if you don't *want* to cook you can develop a total lack of talent for it and burn your hand when you toast a piece of bread. But I assume that, like the vast majority you would like to cook, even if you don't have help. If this is your first party without any help in the kitchen, try a menu of recipes that are simple. None of my recipes are terribly complicated because they are meant for non-cooks or those who feel handicapped with no help. And if a dish isn't perfect the first time, it will be the next time. I am convinced that a lot of that "I simply can't cook" syndrome is due to shyness. One little flop and some people feel doomed. If only they tried again!

Another point: don't try a new dish when you have guests. Inflict it on your family first, or on a couple of close friends. If you live alone, try it on yourself. If you are pleased with the result, attempt it at a party. You'll know you can do it and you will feel secure—very important for your own state of mind.

NO HELP IN
THE PREPARATIONS

Setting the table should be an early priority, no matter what. Set it far ahead of your party at a time when you are calm. Set it early even if it means that your family eats in the kitchen for a couple of evenings or on a small table in another room.

Your table should be complete; a missing item, such as the salt or a soup spoon can ruin a party. Here is my system of preventing that. It has never failed me.

As soon as the tablecloth is straight, I place the plates in their spots, even if I have to remove them again to heat them. Then I place the exact number of spoons, knives, and forks on a sideboard. What is the first piece we are going to use? Soup spoons. I pick them all up and go from one place to the next setting the spoons where they belong. If I am left with one spoon I know I have skipped a place. It is much easier to find the spot where it is missing than to place all the flatware next to one place and go on to the next. Then I add the napkins, the glasses, and the butter plates, if any. I sit down to see if the plate in front of me faces exactly the one across the table; it should, of course.

Then I set down the placecards. (It's really not too much trouble; they actually make life a lot simpler. Have you ever asked your guests to sit wherever they want—only to discover that, apparently, no one wants to sit next to no one? Or that three ladies have plunked themselves down next to each other because, before dinner, they were in the midst of a conversation and wanted to continue it? As you frantically straighten everything out, your first course gets cold.) Placecards save you from all of this. Besides, you know your guests and their interests, and you wouldn't place an ardent golfer next to a woman who doesn't know what a number 2 iron is (and might even consider it rude).

Dorothy Parker, the writer, was once asked what her formula was for a perfect dinner party. "Pretty women and brilliant men," was her answer. (Obviously she did not want brilliant women because she wanted to be the only one.) If you have got them, you have no problem. If you have one bore on your hands, place him so that he can do only a minimum of boring.

NO HELP WITH SERVING

Your food is ready and your table is a joy. When your guests arrive, you are serene.

Even if you had a butler, you would probably pass the appetizers yourself. It is such a nice, welcoming gesture! And it gives you a chance to make people feel at ease, just by dropping a few kind words such as, "How well you look my dear," or "You have lost weight...very becoming," even if none of it is true. After all, you are turning to the next guest and can't be pinned down.

As for drinks, everyone can help him- or herself. Or the men can fix the drinks for the ladies. If you have a husband or a close friend, he can take care of everybody. He would probably want to, but it isn't a must. It has become perfectly acceptable for a lady to pour herself a glass of wine or Scotch on the rocks. (Just as it has become perfectly acceptable not to have the same number of women and men at the table. Only recently I had called a friend to say that my husband wasn't feeling well and that we couldn't come to dinner. "And what is the matter with you? Do you have to stay home to take care of him or are you afraid to go out alone?"

"Neither. He has a cold and I stay away from him. But I don't want to ruin your seating arrangement."

"You are either out of your mind or you think that I am. Get dressed and get yourself over here." She hung up on me and I felt intimidated. Of course I went, and it was a most stimulating evening.)

Very few people will have complicated drinks before dinner. If they do they will also want to fix it themselves. I recently gave one of these no-help dinners, and I knew that one of my female guests was a Martini drinker. I fixed one that I considered perfect, but she refused it. "Have you given up Martinis?" I asked.

"I most certainly have not. But I drink MY Martinis and no one else's." Now I don't bother.

Drinks and appetizers have been taken care of. Now comes dinner and you dread it.

Don't! If you have children over ten, use them. (Though I remember being served by an enchanting eight-year-old redhead and enjoying it.) Of course they won't be perfect, but no one expects them to be. However, avoid having them carry soup bowls filled to the brim, particularly if the soup is hot, but ask them to remove used plates and bring in clean ones. They will probably remove them from the wrong side, and no one will think that you don't know any better. Just don't stare at them and make them nervous. They will drop a plate and it will be your fault!

If you have no children, or they are too small, or they are away at school, place the food on a sideboard. If you don't have one, use a folding table that can be stored out of sight when it isn't in use. Place hot foods on hot trays; they are an excellent investment, and I also use them for everyday dining. Everything except the dessert should be displayed. Then you have two choices: you can have the individual plates on the sideboard and dish out the food for each guest, then have them take it back to their places; or you can say, "Please find your places at the table and then help yourselves."

I opt for the first formula: you remain in control of your party and can see to it that no one dawdles before helping her- or himself. And, very importantly, you can see to it that the ladies don't all help themselves while the men hang back. When this happens, all the ladies are seated, forlornly, while they wait for the men to join them. In the meantime, no one eats and the food gets cold. If you do the serving, you can insist that men and women alternate and start eating.

Pouring the wine seems to be a man's job, only because it is a tradition, mind you. I pour wine better than most men I know but admitting that makes me sound un-feminine. So let's leave the pouring to one of your male guests, hoping that he knows how to give the bottle that little twist at the end so that you don't have a lot of red wine spots on your tablecloth. (If you do, don't be unhappy. Remember that the Chinese feel that they are the sign of a good party.) And your party *is* good.

When the time comes for clearing the table and serving the dessert, you get up and—maybe—your closest friend. But allow no one else, no matter how they insist "we will all help." It would only interrupt the conversation, and make a mess in your kitchen. I much prefer to remove all the plates myself, if only to prevent someone else's stacking the used plates with leftovers on them. What a mess to clean up before putting them in the dishwasher! If a friend helps you, tell her "don't stack!"

For the dessert, you have two choices: you can place the plates in front of each guest and have them pass the bowl of fruit or the platter with the cake from one to another. Or you can have the plates next to you, the dessert in front of you, and you can place a portion on each plate, then pass them along. It somewhat depends on what you are serving.

As for coffee, set up a tray ahead of time in the kitchen and then bring it in when you are ready. Whether you wish to serve it at the dinner table or in the living room or in some other corner of the apartment is up to you. Only—please—don't serve it *with* the dessert, but after. It's called after-dinner coffee, remember?

I fight a constant battle with waiters in restaurants who bring the coffee while I am still enjoying my last sip of wine with my dessert. If I don't complain, they plunk the coffee down next to me and—when I am ready to drink it—it's cold.

If the conversation is good, I hate to interrupt it and I bring the coffee to the table. If I feel that some guests should talk to someone other than their dinner companion, I shift the scene to another spot.

NO HELP WITH CLEANING UP

As for cleaning up, there are two kinds of people: the ones who just want to take their clothes off, brush their teeth, and fall into bed—they will face the mess tomorrow—and the ones who can't close an eye until the living room is straightened up—they are the compulsive cleaners. I am somewhere in the middle.

I *have* to rinse the plates and place them in the dishwasher, and I *have* to empty ashtrays. The smell of stale tobacco is more than I can stand. I have, however, no feeling about pots and pans. If they are cluttering up the kitchen to the point that my husband wouldn't have space to make his breakfast the next morning I have been known to wipe them out with paper towels and put them in the oven (cold oven, that is). The scouring can wait.

The glasses can go in the machine the next day.

One thing I like to do is open a window a crack, if it isn't too cold or terribly hot. A large group of people, no matter how soigné, leave a scent behind—a thing I can do without. But before leaving the window open, make sure it is safe, lest you emerge in the morning to find your friendly neighborhood mugger sitting at your kitchen table eating your leftovers.

Lastly, if you can possibly afford to have someone come in the next day to do a professional cleaning job you will be a lot happier. I know I would be.

NO HOST

This is a problem that baffles me. Why is it that an intelligent, independent woman who wouldn't hesitate to go alone on a trip around the world, feels that a husband—even if he were useless and without much personality—is a necessity at a dinner party?

Without a husband, some women's confidence seems to vanish, almost as if a husband were an indispensable status symbol. It is somewhat like the famous initials on a tee-shirt.

A woman recently divorced mentioned to me that she was not getting invited to dinners anymore. She found it quite plausible, though she was obviously hurt.

"Who would invite a woman alone?" she said.

I agree that people find it easier to invite couples, though most hostesses seem quite able to find a dinner companion for a single woman. Not only, but people seem to care less and less about having an equal number of men and women at dinner. However, it also seemed to me that, when she was first divorced there were quite a few invitations.

"Yes, in the beginning, because people felt sorry for me, then they got tired of that single woman. I became a nuisance."

It didn't occur to her that people might not have gotten tired of the single woman, but of continuing to invite someone who never invited them back. I said so, as tactfully as I knew how, which wasn't *very* tactful.

She replied with an avalanche of excuses. "I have no time." (I have heard that excuse so often that I have grown a little tired of it.) "I am a poor cook." "My patients keep me too busy." (She is a doctor.) I pointed out that she was a poor cook also when she was married, and yet she inflicted her cooking on guests; that she had patients also when she was married, and yet found the time for some entertaining; and finally that she still had weekends when she was not on call.

It was all to no avail. She obviously had always hated to entertain, even when she had a husband, and now without one she simply couldn't face it. This brilliant, self-asserting woman, who had always interrupted her husband when he tried to tell a story, told me she wouldn't know how to keep a conversation going without a husband.

I feel deeply sorry for women like her (and there are many), though I get somewhat impatient. They could pull themselves together and entertain, starting perhaps with a small group of long-time friends.

The only problem is that many divorced women want their old friends to take sides. If friends as much as still nod to their "ex-"

they feel betrayed and they "are out." This is a terrible thing to do to one's friends and to oneself, but this is an emotional problem and I mention it here only because it makes life in general—and entertaining in particular—so much more complicated.

Let us assume that the divorced lady has overcome her bitterness to the extent that she can bring herself to invite a few friends. She will find that people will accept with great pleasure, even if they had other plans for that evening. They will realize that, at that point in her life, any "sorry, dear, but we have other plans" would feel like a rejection to her.

Everybody will come, and everybody will be in high spirits, sensing her tension. Not a word will be said about her divorce, nor about her no-longer-better-half. There will be high praise for the way she has redone the apartment; the men will fix the drinks, the women will serve the appetizers. It will all be like a big, happy family. The evening will be a success and it will give the hostess quite a lift. It will also give her the feeling that she wants to get back into some sort of social life.

This particular lady found a very clever formula. She learned to prepare one dish to perfection. The dish is easy, it may be prepared ahead of time, and it requires nothing but a salad and a dessert to make it a perfect meal. This isn't a dish for sophisticated gourmets, but is tasty and looks inviting; it is a meat pie (see page 216). When she first described it to me I winced a little (not so that she saw it), but when I tried it I had to admit that I liked it.

Since she doesn't always serve it to the same people she can continue with her limited repertory for quite awhile. "Actually I can probably go on forever with my one menu. I don't entertain that often, and once a year everybody can endure my meatpie."

She is, of course, quite right. In fact she has learned to make a joke of it: "Are you ready for another meatpie?" she would ask when she invites people. And most of them are. She adds a large green salad, for which she uses excellent olive oil, and serves a chocolate mousse for dessert. The latter comes right out of a how-to-use-your-food-processor booklet and presents no problem.

Cheese Topped with Polenta, page 173

She has fine china and silver, and has learned to use them. Her table looks lovely and she enjoys it. So do her guests. She is still not crazy about entertaining, but she has found a pattern and feels secure with it. And that is as important for a good party as the food itself.

WIDOWS

Widows have a different problem. They don't have to overcome bitterness—only loneliness.

Friends tend to have more compassion for widows than for divorced women. It's unjust and few would admit it, but somewhere—and maybe only in their subconscious—people say in the case of a divorcée, "it must have been her fault too." Maybe it was, but that still doesn't change the fact that her life is shattered and that her ex-husband will probably find it easier to re-build his life than she does hers.

Anyway, there are no qualms or doubts about a widow. She is alone, she is unhappy, and our hearts go out to her. The best thing we can do for her is make her feel less alone.

I feel that one should never drop in on anyone. Even a person who longs for company has moments when she would rather be alone. But I guess at times we all have called a friend and said, "I find myself with an enormous beef stew that we can't possibly eat up. May I bring you some? In case you want to have a couple of friends in." The offer might not always be accepted, but the recipient of the call feels better for it.

But this mood of ours won't last too long. After a couple of months we expect a woman to find her bearing and start living again. That doesn't mean that she won't hurt, but it does mean that she won't show it so much. It's a horrible thing to have to admit, but we all tire of tears.

A particularly brave friend of mine said almost as soon as she lost her husband, "My tears are a private thing between my pillow and myself." None of us has ever seen her cry. On the surface she is as much fun as she ever was and that is quite a bit. And she has never let herself go. She doesn't overeat or overdrink, and her figure has remained perfect. "I have lost my audience," she says, "but I still dress for him."

But—she hates to cook! I don't think I have ever known anyone who so looked at a kitchen as if it were a torture chamber. She is a marvelous driver and says she could drive 1,000 miles and would be less tired than she is after boiling an egg. Yet she realized that she had to learn if she ever wanted company. And she does.

She is among the lucky ones who have someone who does the cleaning, but cooking is another matter. She too felt that if she learned to make one dish perfectly she would be like an actress who is good in one part and people keep going to see her.

She chose eggs Benedict, which she loves. She wanted to prove to me how good she was, and I was to stand beside her while she made the Hollandaise sauce, provided I didn't speak because it would confuse her. There was not a peep out of me while I stood and watched that poor woman struggle with a double boiler and she cut into the butter as if it were the enemy. It was pathetic, and I must have moved.

"Now you have ruined everything," she said. "I am sure it is going to curdle." It didn't. And the eggs were edible, though she had poached them in a poacher instead of the preferable whirlpool of boiling water.

"I think I will go and lie down," she said after that ordeal, looking limp.

I told her that she had chosen one of the most difficult dishes to prepare, which is only half true but it cheered her up. Then I started to teach her a few very simple recipes.

First I taught her how to cook rice: how to boil it, I mean. "When I boil rice it becomes a sort of white glue," she had said; apparently she boiled it in very little water and for as long as the poor rice would stand it.

Then I taught her how to make several rice salads (pages 185–187). I showed her how to make a good salad dressing, and I even taught her a simple dessert that can be made well ahead of time. I don't know whether she attempted the dessert; my guess is that she bought desserts ready made. But I do know that the rice salads almost became her trademark!

She is an avid card player and enjoys entertaining friends for bridge. She would set up a small buffet with a rice salad and a green salad. When a player got carried away by hunger, he or she got up and fixed a little something to eat. I don't say that this is the ideal way to entertain, but this hostess chose it and her friends enjoy it; it suits their life-style.

REASONS FOR ENTERTAINING

There are divorced or widowed women who simply can't face the idea of picking up the pieces and continue to live as they did before. If they can afford to, they go on long trips to weird and wonderful countries where nothing reminds them of their previous existence. They hope, of course, that on top of the camel to their left will suddenly appear the man of their future. This man seldom materializes, but even if the lady comes back alone she will bring with her some marvelous films or photos. These are a great excuse to invite people for an evening.

"I have some wonderful pictures to show you. Why don't you come and we can look at them and then we have a bite."

This takes the emphasis away from the food. But not only that—it also doesn't require the presence of a host. In fact, he might be a nuisance. While she might want to show her guests the flowers at Windsor Castle or the sunset on the Nile, he might prefer they understand the efficiency of the boiler room on the ship. And whether you have an equal number of men and women is totally unimportant if you have gotten together to admire travel pictures.

But don't overdo the pictures; feed your guests too. A buffet from which everybody helps him- or herself can be as simple or as elabo-

rate as you choose. Cold cuts, nicely arranged on several small platters and accompanied by small dishes of olives and radishes, flanked
by a large green salad and a variety of good crusty breads, makes a
great buffet. Follow that with a bowl of fresh fruit and maybe cookies if you are a baker. Such a party is certainly no problem, nor does
it require a host.

I have a friend who has entertained without a host for quite a few
years now. But even when she was shattered because her husband
had walked out on her she kept entertaining.

Granted: she is a privileged person. Not only is she stunning, she
also has a delightful apartment that she has decorated with great
taste. She has a roof terrace and, as she is a most talented gar-
dener, it is an oasis in the big city. And that is where she mostly
entertains.

The first thing she did when she found herself alone was to take a
cooking course. She had a job, but she went to cooking school at
night. It was well worth the effort. She is a superb cook, and her
little outdoor dinners are among the most successful in town. No
one misses the host; he was a bore anyway, even when he was
around.

She usually serves a cold soup to begin (pages 140–141), followed
by a cold fish or a cold meat dish and a very simple dessert. Most of
it is prepared the evening before because she doesn't get home
from work much before her guests arrive.

I was there recently and admired plates I had not seen before. They
are pure white and have a scalloped edge. "I bought them on sale
for very little," she said. "I had felt for some time that my china was
too loud for outdoors, with all that greenery around."

I had never minded the other china, but I had to admit that the
green and white setting made for a deliciously serene evening. It
was serene even on an evening when the soup got a bit diluted
because it rained while we were eating. The women put the napkins
over their heads, and by the time the meat arrived it had stopped
raining.

SINGLE WOMEN

How about single women? Women who have never married and maybe don't intend to. How do they cope without a host?

I had a long talk with a brilliant, cheerful woman in her late thirties. How does she handle the problem?

"What problem?" she asked.

"Entertaining without a host."

She looked at me as if there were something wrong with my head.

"Look, that's no problem. Never has been. Sure, I sometimes have a bunch of friends up and I might ask a man to fix the drinks or to get the ice out. But mostly to make him feel good, not because I can't do it myself. I think we single women are the luckiest hostesses because we don't feel that we have to impress someone. I might ask people for hotdogs and beer and it's okay. And, if I wanted to spend the money, I could ask them for caviar and champagne and it would also be okay. But don't take my word for it: talk to some other single women and see what they tell you."

I did and they all agreed with the first.

One of them is active in her church. The friends she made there go from almost penniless students to wealthy, stately matrons. They all like my friend and, as she lives pretty close to the church, they come by after Sunday service for a drink, a snack, and a chat.

She doesn't have much money, but that's no problem. Someone might bring a bottle of wine or a can of crabmeat. She is a very good cook and has invented a rice salad with seafood (see page 187) that has become quite famous. (Her friends see to it that she always is well equipped with fine olive oil.) Nor would she hesitate to prepare her dish while her guests are there.

She has lovely dishes and very good silver and uses both, but she doesn't have much space. Platters and bowls are stored under the evening gowns in her closet, which does not bother her one bit. And it is precisely her relaxed attitude that makes her so popular.

NO HOSTESS

Of all the problems considered in this book, this is the least problematic. After all, no one expects things to be perfect when the host is a bachelor, whether that state be temporary or permanent. What is clumsy when a woman makes a mistake (Heavens! You'd think she would know how to make a roast!) becomes endearing when a man does it. (Isn't he charming, the way he is trying to cope all by himself?)

Dozens of hands are ready, willing, and some even able to come to the bachelor's aid. And it makes no difference whether he is a very young man who is trying to throw the first party of his life, or an elderly one who has suddenly gotten tired of restaurants or has realized that they cost too much.

Some men are, of course, superb cooks. In fact—and at the risk of making a lot of female enemies—a man who understands cuisine is often a better cook than a woman. I know some whose dinners could make gastronomic history and, for the reason I have given above, they are less fussy than women tend to be. What does it matter if he has forgotten the salad forks or if there are no finger bowls? He doesn't mind and neither do his guests, which makes for a relaxed, cozy atmosphere.

"Sit wherever you want," the host will say, as he emerges from the kitchen in shirt sleeves, with a big apron tied around himself, carrying a hugh wooden board that holds a magnificent roast or leg of lamb. He will carve it to perfection and serve it with a flourish. With a huge kitchen fork he will pick up the potatoes and the vegetables. Then he will take off his apron, throw it into some corner of the room, and sit down. If there are no salt or pepper on the table, he will get up and get them without feeling self-conscious.

How many of us have enough self-assurance to put on a similar performance? How many of us would not say, "Oh dear! I have forgotten the pepper!" and look all flustered and make everybody feel guilty for wanting pepper? But this chapter is not intended for men who know how to entertain and do it with great ease. It is for the vast majority who are totally thrown by the idea of entertaining. They don't know how to market, except for their own bacon and eggs. Their table, assuming that they have one, is covered with yesterday's newspaper, a couple of magazines, and papers from the IRS.

GETTING STARTED

Throw out everything except the papers from the IRS. If you can't throw out anything, place it all in a folder and hide it—under the bed, if you must. It will do wonders for your room. If you have a tablecloth, spread it over the table. If not, see to it that you have enough placemats for the number of guests you have invited. (Remember that mats take up more space than a cloth. If you can seat eight with a cloth, you can probably seat only six with mats.)

Make sure you have a fork, a knife, and maybe a spoon for each guest, but don't worry too much about how to place them. The knife goes to the right of the plate and the fork to the left. But if you then don't know what to do with the spoon, place both the knife and the fork to the left, and put the spoon to the right. Your guests will know what to do with them.

The napkins should go with the forks, but, unless you are really ambitious, don't worry about how to fold them. There is an entire book on napkin folding, but it is neither for beginners nor for people who have other things to do in life. (I assume that our would-be host is working.)

Think carefully about what you want to serve and stick to it. Don't get carried away by something weird and wonderful that you see in the market that day, thinking "I might as well try this." And don't try anything new! Stick to things you have cooked before and know you can handle. Be sure of the quantities you need.

Supposing you want to serve a steamed chicken (see page 202). It is very simple to make and may be prepared the day before; also, the vegetables are built-in. It's an ideal dish, particularly in winter. (Actually I don't know why winter. Maybe it is because there is something heartwarming about a large platter with a steaming chicken, surrounded by hot vegetables.)

The only problem is that a chicken, cooked whole, is a little complicated to serve. Don't get fancy or creative with it! I recall a bachelor who once tried to carve a chicken as if it were a turkey. The poor bird was cut into unappetizing bits and slivers, while the wing tips clung to denuded bones. Carried away by his own dexterity, the host cut into his own thumb; it was not attractive and we all munched a lot of bread instead and drank a lot of his excellent wine.

But you won't do that. You will remove the tail end and the wing tips in the kitchen. Then place the steamed chicken on a platter and surround it with the vegetables if the platter is large enough. You will find such a dish in every French or Italian country kitchen. Place it in front of you at the table with an empty bowl or platter next to it into which you will transfer the vegetables before cutting up the chicken. If you try to do it while the vegetables are in your way, you may be sure that a carrot will fly across the room when you least expect it.

Cut the wings off, then the drumsticks; quarter the rest. Ask each guest what part he or she wants and, if you are lucky, they won't all want the same.

Try holding a dress rehearsal a few days before the party. Boil a smaller chicken for yourself or, at most, for one other friend. When the evening of the dinner comes, you will know exactly how to cut the bird with finesse.

Men don't have to worry about appetizers. Nuts and potato chips are all that is expected of them. If a man were to prepare dainty little sandwiches, he would seem almost ridiculous.

Nor does he have to worry about an elaborate dessert. Fruit and cheese are perfect. But if you really want to be different, don't make the cheese a brie. Brie is a perfectly good cheese. The trouble is only that it is "in" and people who know nothing about cheeses, and who don't make the effort to learn about them, unfailingly will buy and serve brie. It's safe! At times they don't even bother to find out if it is ripe or not.

I recently heard from a lady who had been uncommonly kind to her cleaning woman, helping her with family problems that would otherwise have required the hiring of a lawyer. At Christmastime, the cleaning woman wanted to express her gratitude; she bought her employer a wheel of brie. She had obviously asked someone in a cheese store what cheese would make a good impression.

If you want to be a little more imaginative, in addition to making a good impression, discuss cheeses with the person behind the counter in a really good cheese store. And try a few. Buy some for yourself and eat them with fruit. Educate your own palate and then trust it. You will not only add to the enjoyment of your guests but also to your own.

MOVING ON

Is the steamed chicken too banal? There are all sorts of other fascinating chicken dishes. Still too common? Well, if you find that entertaining is fun and decide that you want to do more of it, invest in a chafing dish. If you want to be really trendy, get a wok. Once you learn how to use either, you will find it easy and fun. What's more, if you are a "ham," these tools will allow you to give a splendid performance, particularly if your kitchen is in plain view and you can be part of the conversation while you cook. But again, practice using your chafing dish without guests first. And try the wok a couple of times before showing it off for company. You have to get used to it, but also a wok needs to be seasoned. And for your first dinners, choose the easiest among the recipes for a wok or chafing dish. Master two or three of these and become famous for them: "your specialty," as it were.

Actually, you can cook many oriental dishes without a wok and still offer your guests unusual but simple-to-prepare meals. With or without a wok, Chinese food has a great advantage over most other foods: very few people are such experts as to be able to criticize you for not doing it right. Also you can say very nonchalantly, "I picked this recipe up in a little restaurant in Peking."

I actually find Chinese cooking easy, tasty, and quite glamorous. What more does a host want? One more thing. This food lends itself to pretty implements: pretty bowls, white porcelain spoons, and of course the chance to show off your ability with chopsticks (if indeed you have that ability).

A very attractive bachelor who travels widely and frequently confessed to me the other day that the one thing that destroys his pleasure in traveling in China is chopsticks. (How I feel for him! For some reason, I have never been able to master them.) When he last went to China he took with him a beautiful silver fork, which he put in his pocket whenever he went to a restaurant. It turned out to be the best trip ever, with most enjoyable meals. And the Chinese loved his fork. Maybe your guests will be much happier with forks too.

Another good thing about Chinese cooking is that all the ingredients can be chopped or sliced ahead of time, with only the sautéeing done at the last moment, perhaps in front of your guests. If you choose to do it this way, arrange the ingredients on a tray (possibly lacquer) in multicolored stripes. Very decorative! When the time comes to do the actual cooking, just pick up a handful of finely chopped Chinese cabbage, another handful of sliced water chestnuts, and whatever else the recipe requires, and then nonchalantly throw everything in succession into the wok or skillet and stir-fry until done. Very theatrical! Very effective!

If cooking in front of guests doesn't appeal to you there is the old stand-by—the casserole. Or try the more recently popular rice salad or pasta salad; both can be turned into main courses.

If you don't care for oriental food but want to stick to Western, you will need something to end the meal. (Oriental food should really be followed only by fruit or, at most, a sherbet.) Cheese is, of course, always a good idea. I have already expressed my feelings about the ubiquitous brie. Why not try a cheese that has only recently become popular: goat cheese. There are many different types, from mild to pungent, and in my opinion they are all delicious.

Some time ago I visited an American friend who was temporarily living in Paris. He spoke no French, no matter how hard he tried. He took me to Paris' most famous restaurant and, being a snob, he asked me to order a really fancy dessert—something that would make the headwaiter stand at attention and let him know that we were really "in the know."

I asked the man, "How about a good Chèvre?" Literally, "How about a good goat?"

The waiter disappeared and my friend looked disappointed and almost angry. "You really *had* to let me down, didn't you?" he asked. Only when the waiter and I got into a lively conversation about the merits of this cheese over the other, did he cheer up.

A good chèvre is quite a delicacy and has a strong gastronomic following. It goes marvelously with fresh pears. But it is, however, a pungent cheese and might not appeal to someone who has never tasted it. I would advise also serving a mild back-up cheese.

Even if the host is strictly a Bourbon drinker he has to know enough about wine to serve it properly. He knows, of course, that red wine goes with dark meats and white with chicken, veal, fish, and certain egg dishes. He also knows that white wine should be chilled and red served at room temperature. But I would like to add a few things. First, the rule about red with one thing and white with another isn't all that strict. Except perhaps for venison and some serious beef dishes, it is perfectly acceptable to serve white wine if the guests prefer it. And you won't become an outcast if you like a light red wine with your chicken.

As for the temperature, don't *over*chill the white, particularly if it is a noble Burgundy. And, if you are drinking a young red wine—say a young Chianti or a Beaujolais—it should rather be at cellar temperature than at the temperature of your living room which might be 80 degrees. If you are a beginner, keep in mind that wine which is to be served with food should be dry. If you see the words *semisweet* or *abbocato* on the bottle stay away from it. Personally I also avoid wines that tell you that they are mellow. What this usually means is that they are not dry enough.

At the conclusion of your dinner—after dessert—you will want to serve coffee. Men being privileged, instant coffee is permissible. And a man may serve it in large cups. In fact, a man who tries to cope with dainty little cups might even be a bit silly.

OTHER MATTERS

Another thing a man doesn't seem to have to worry about much is the tidiness of his home or apartment. Of course it shouldn't be dirty, and the bathroom should be in good shape, complete with guest towels (could be paper). But do give some thought to how things look to your guests.

I remember a dinner in the house of a young bachelor. He was one of those men who is an excellent cook. And the dinner was truly superb. He also collects art. When he told us that he had acquired a new painting, we all asked to see it. When he said that it hung in the bedroom, we still asked to see it. When he said that his bedroom was a mess, we really insisted!

And a mess it was. A huge antique bed hadn't been made, a pair of pajamas had been flung across the room and had landed only partway on a chair, the slippers stood pigeon-toed in a corner as if they had been punished. The host explained various points of the painting to us, which was beautiful. He was totally at ease in the messy surrounding. He had warned us, hadn't he?

The ladies exchanged smiling glances. There wasn't one of us who wouldn't gladly have helped him straighten up the room. I was even told later that one of the ladies had offered to make the mess worse—later in the evening when the rest of us had gone home!

Would a woman dare take guests into a messy bedroom? Not even if she had bought the *Mona Lisa* and wanted to show her off.

There is another problem particularly relevant to this chapter: what does the single man do with his guests' coats—or at times even with overshoes? His so-called guest closet is probably full to bursting and is best not even opened, lest a pair of skis fall on the heads of guests.

Assuming that the bed is made, coats can be placed on it, possibly the men's coats first and the ladies' on top of them. Overshoes go in the bathroom, where they can drip without causing damage.

Some last advice: don't take it all too seriously—it's only a dinner party! If something goes wrong (and something sometimes does, even for the most skillful party-giver), don't say "I simply can't do it and I shall never try again." Try to analyze what went wrong and avoid that next time. If you have problems with the food, practice your recipes before serving them to guests. If your timing was off, and your cocktail time was too long, don't allow so much time for that next time. Did your food get cold? Serve it on hot trays in the future and encourage your guests to begin eating as soon as served. When you know what went wrong, you'll avoid that next time. The first time you manage a truly successful party, you will feel like a king.

NO COURAGE

T here seem to be two types of people who have no courage when it comes to giving parties: those who entertain frequently and do so because they can't stand being alone, and those who prefer being alone and cringe at the very thought of entertaining their friends. Let's look first at the gregarious ones.

"GREAT" HOSTESSES

Some women are not even aware of being bothered by doubts and apprehensions about their own parties. Outwardly they seem assured and in control, but suddenly you realize that they needed a tranquilizer before their guests arrived.

A woman I know quite well is an avid party-giver. Whether she enjoys her parties I can't really tell, but she seems to get terribly upset if people keep talking when a new dish is served. All conversation should be interrupted until the guests have a chance to admire the platter and have expressed that admiration. The trouble is that it isn't easy to pick up a conversation when it has been dropped so suddenly.

I was once present when she actually interrupted a very good story someone was telling, as she demanded that her guests look at a platter of mixed vegetables "while it is still beautiful." That command destroyed the person's story, but it didn't matter to her; after all, it wasn't *her* story.

The story never did get finished—the conversation had lost its lilt. The guests looked into their plates and seemed a trifle embarrassed. After dinner she said to me, "You do understand, don't you? After all I had been through?"

After all she had been through?

She was giving another dinner party shortly after the other, and she had asked me to come by during the day. It seemed an odd moment but I thought she might have something urgent to discuss with me.

She didn't. She just talked and talked while the house was quivering with servants. One was frantically arranging flowers. Another was anxiously placing fresh candles into candlesticks. The whole atmosphere was un-serene to say the least, and I could not wait to get out of there.

"Don't go yet," she said grabbing my arm. "You must have a million things to do," I said, getting up.

"All I have to do is write the placecards and make the seating arrangement. And I dread it so that I am happy to have an excuse to delay doing it."

I was so surprised I couldn't blink.

"What is so frightening about a seating arrangement?" I finally asked.

"Suppose someone feels slighted. Or I seat someone next to a person he or she doesn't get along with? It's a nightmare." She frantically knocked on wood and added, "Thank heaven, so far I have been doing alright."

If she had been a very young hostess with no experience I could have understood—maybe! But she was not a young woman, and she had given hundreds of dinner parties. Apparently if one considers entertaining an ordeal, years of experience won't make it less so.

The funny thing is that such people don't know they are anxious about entertaining. They want to be considered great hostesses, and they entertain all the time—in agony! If one were to ask them, "Why?" the answer would be, "Well, that's my life."

Very recently I ran into a man I have known for a long time. He is handsome, he is temporarily unattached, and he has excellent manners and a good name. He is, of course, constantly pursued by "great" hostesses.

"Will you talk to me for a minute?" he said.

"Sure."

"What is it with them? Why do they give these parties? Only to dress up? No one seems to enjoy them, heaven knows. The hostess is unfailingly tense, the guests bored or bitchy. And now they all blame me because I refuse those dreadful invitations. Well, I do prefer reading a book, or playing poker with some chums. Is that so hard to understand? I have made more enemies in these last few months than I have made in my whole life, I think."

He really started me thinking about all those people who entertain constantly, suffering and making other people suffer. I think the reason is that they can't be alone; the idea of spending an evening by themselves is unendurable. It certainly isn't that they long to see the people they invite; they see them all the time anyway. But they look at their engagement books, and there is an evening with nothing to do that stares them in the face. They can't stand it, so they make a few phone calls.

That's the reason they entertain, but why do they dread it so? Why is arranging a dinner party such an ordeal? I have asked myself this over and over. My reasoning might be totally wrong, but I think it is because they have—basically—nothing to offer.

If you suddenly realize that you haven't seen the Smiths in a long time, and that brings to mind that you miss the Martins, whom you like a lot and never see, and the Gleasons, and so on and so on, that makes for a party. That's fine; in fact, it is very good. But that is not the way they operate. They want to give a party, and they go through their book to find the names of people to invite. They do and—as the day arrives—they get scared. What if the party is a bore? What if people start going home early? If only there were one person they could count on to be brilliant or at least witty. But they usually can't.

And there is something else. That kind of hostess usually doesn't know anything about food. If she did, and knew that the food would be exceptional and that people would love it and comment on it, she would feel quite secure. As food conscious as this country is nowadays, a hostess who serves truly great meals is a successful hostess. But these ladies don't.

I remember an evening, some time ago, when I had gone early to the house of a woman I know, to give her a hand with last-minute arrangements. (Or to hold her hand, as I later realized.) At the first ring of the door bell she took a swig (and I mean a SWIG) of brandy.

"That is going to ruin your palate," I said. "You won't be able even to taste the food."

"Don't care about food," she muttered and put on her brave and impeccable smile. Poor thing.

SHY HOSTESS

And then there is the hostess who knows that she has no courage. She is always looking for excuses.

"I really have to plan a party. I owe dozens of people! Unfortunately, I can't do anything this month. Aunt Elizabeth is coming from San Francisco and I don't exactly know when. She might show up any minute."

Nonsense! I know Aunt Elizabeth. She would never arrive without fair warning. Not only that, but she is a handsome, youngish woman, is very gregarious, and would be delighted if her hosts had a party. Besides, next month my friend would find another excuse not to give that party. She wouldn't really admit it or want to talk about her fears, so there is no use convincing her.

In the case of my friend, even all her husband's urgings were getting him nowhere. Apparently he finally realized what the situation really was and decided to take matters into his own hands. He simply picked a date and started inviting people. If his wife were the type of woman who would wring her hands, she would have done so. But she isn't that type, so she called me.

"Do you know what that b____ is doing? He is inviting people! I think he has about twenty now, and he is still inviting. I pretend I don't know it. If he wants to have a party, let him do the marketing, let him find the help, let him...."

"And what are you going to do the night of the party?" I inquired as calmly as I could. "Go to the movies? Wait at the corner until the guests have left and sneak back into your apartment? Do you want J____ to say 'my wife is too dumb or too inept to give a party, so I am giving one'?"

"What do you suggest?"

"That you pull yourself together and start planning the party. Begin by thinking about the menu."

"Will you help me?"

"You know I will."

So I went to their apartment, which is perfectly beautiful—or could be. I found her in the kitchen in the same state of despair she had been in when we spoke on the phone. The kitchen was the size of a respectable ballroom. All the cabinets that hold the china and the crystal were opened.

"Some of these things have never been used. I don't even know what is in these cabinets."

"It is about time we found out." (I find that, if you use the pronoun *we* rather than *you*, it makes timid people feel less alone in this cruel world and it gives them courage.)

I climbed up a ladder and started to take down plate after plate, platter after platter, and bowls of all sizes. Some were good and others were perfectly magnificent. The best pieces had been inherited from their families, and some were also wedding presents. I love beautiful china, and my eyes sparkled. But the beauty of it all was lost on this woman.

"And you never use these?" I asked, holding up a pale blue Royal Worcester plate that could make the heart sing.

She shrugged. "'course not. Too much trouble."

I glanced at what was obviously the everyday china near the sink, and suddenly this bright woman who has been my close friend for years seemed a stranger. I tried to tell her how beautiful her possessions are but I got no reaction.

"And now we are going to wash all of this and count how many plates you have; it might be enough for a dinner for thirty. None of it goes into the dishwasher, at least not while I am looking."

There followed quite an argument. If you know how to load a dishwasher, so that plates don't knock against each other, they could all go into the dishwasher—that was her opinion. I explained to her about glazes, and how the hot water with the detergents can't help but destroy the colors and the golden edges.

I think I got to her. She held a particularly beautiful plate in her hands for awhile, and she *saw* it for the first time. She seemed to realize that it was pretty.

We soaked the plates in warm suds. They had the dust of ages on them. Then we went through the apartment to see what else she needed to rent. All that was necessary was tables and chairs. The apartment was spacious and potentially beautiful, but it was obviously unloved and showed it.

I know of a wholesale flower market, and that is where I dragged the poor woman the day before the party. We returned to her place—in a cab full of flowers—and filled all the vases, some of which had never been used before. I think she liked the result.

The next day I was there, bright and early. I had, of course, realized that it would be foolish to plan an elaborate dinner with a lot of foods she was not comfortable with. But the woman's kitchen had an indoor barbecue with a chimney over it. I had suggested we have small individual steaks (she had winced at the cost, but I pointed out to her that it was once every ten years), enormous bowls of green salad, baked potatoes, and a dessert. It was easy to serve and, by asking each guest "rare or well done?" and remembering who wanted what, we would give the party a personal touch.

We had two people to serve, and they were quite good, although they had their hands full. To lessen the load, I told them to place the salad bowls next to one guest at each table, for the guests to pass to one another; it worked well.

The butler had wanted to show off and insisted on slowly and carefully pouring the wine, with the result that some people would have finished their meat before getting any wine. Instead, I insisted that one man at each table would take care of the wine.

The party was successful. While coffee was served in the living room, I went back to the dining room and, with the help of the maid, folded and removed the tables and chairs. The guests then danced to the music of some marvelous records the hosts owned.

As I left, the hostess said to me, "You know, this was actually fun?"

Shy hostesses have only one thing in common with "great" hostesses: a fear of parties. Aside from that, their lives are usually the exact opposite. They often lead full and fascinating existences, and they are good at whatever work they do. Once they overcome their initial misgivings, they are excellent hostesses. They usually have read (or written) a new book no one else had read, or they have interviewed someone fascinating (or have been interviewed), or have seen the latest show in town. In other words, they contribute to the conversation, and they also usually invite interesting people.

Women such as my reluctant friend are not at all afraid of spending an evening alone at home. They love to read, they enjoy listening to music. But if they are not careful, they will suddenly realize that they are spending too many evenings alone. Books and records are great but they cannot take the place of a group of congenial friends.

I remember the words of a great man, Carl van Doren: "If you want friendship you have to endure a little boredom."

A CHANGE FROM
THE USUAL

I n earlier chapters of this book I have given some suggestions for more unusual types of parties but have concentrated mainly on dinner parties, whether they be buffet style or sit-down affairs. But now let's consider some of the many other possibilities of entertaining—conventional and not so conventional.

PICNICS

They say that life is no picnic, and obviously this means that it isn't all fun and games. But picnics can be very enjoyable, and preparing for them can also be fun.

I love picnics, especially the preparations for them. Perhaps the only exception to this is a picnic on the beach, which sounds so romantic but always results in sand in your food. The best time to picnic on the beach is in the late evening, when the sand is damp and won't blow in your face; but I don't especially like sitting on wet sand, do you?

Excluding beaches, you can have picnics in all sorts of places—even indoors. Although the dictionary indicates that a picnic is a "pleasure party...where the food is eaten outdoors," I think it is any meal that is not eaten in the usual dining room, at the usual table, sitting on the usual chairs.

I know a couple: she was a widow and he a widower. They were "going together" for a while before they got married. Each had an apartment. Some evenings they would dine at her place and other times at his; and some evenings they would picnic. She had a huge, low coffee table in her living room, and she would pile all the cushions she could find at the two ends. She'd place two candelabra on the floor, and they would "picnic" in the living room, sitting on the floor. And other nights they would "picnic" in some corner of his apartment. She would bring the food, he would supply the wine. They have been married now for several years, and they always eat in the dining room, at the usual table, in the usual chairs. Pity.

But going back to conventional outdoor picnics, don't you long for them as soon as the weather gets warm and friendly? And don't you long to make them less conventional?

The possibilities are endless. A year or so ago, a small group wanted to celebrate the birthday of a friend of ours. It was early June, and the weather was flawless. We decided to have lunch in a park (a public park, that is) not too far from the center of town. It would not be in one of those horrid picnic areas that always seem to smell of someone else's hot dogs. All we wanted was a lawn, possibly not strewn with greasy papers. And we were lucky. No one except us seemed to want a lawn without benches or tables. There were no papers and not a soul in sight.

I brought three blankets, which I spread out to form a triangle. We were six, and each blanket would "seat" two people comfortably. The space in the center we covered with an old but very colorful tablecloth. You need to protect your cloths more carefully at a picnic. Instead of dainty napkins, I had brought kitchen towels that somewhat matched the cloth. I had also brought placecards, which the lightest breeze blew away; they were obviously superfluous.

The small bunch of very short-stemmed flowers were not superfluous, however. I placed them in a small container that I then put in the center of the cloth. They added a touch. But the real hit of the party were my two ice buckets. I had placed a bottle of champagne in each and packed shaved ice around them. The ice survived beautifully and also made the bottles stand up straight. I had also brought along some crystal goblets (stemware won't stand up on a lawn) to avoid the incongruous combination of champagne and plastic. Nothing got broken! Not even the plates, which were pottery.

The flatware, however, was stainless steel, partly because it's quite handsome and partly because it seemed safer these days not to use silver out in the open.

The others brought the food: long loaves of crusty bread that we broke instead of cutting; various salads in tight containers which don't spill; strong cheeses (no worry about smelling up the outdoors); a small birthday cake; and a huge thermos of coffee. We even had mints.

It was one of the best parties any of us had ever been to. Granted, we were a congenial group and would probably also have had a good time had we gone to a restaurant or to someone's house. But we wouldn't have felt so carefree—as if we had all shed a few years. The only setback was when the group started singing; I, forgetting what a terrible voice I have, joined in and it broke up the party!

That was a very special party, and we all wanted it to be festive, but a couple of bottles of white wine would have been perfectly adequate instead of champagne. Make sure that for all picnics you don't bring too much food. With the price of food being what it is, no one wants to throw out what does not get eaten, and there is nothing more difficult than re-wrapping leftovers at a picnic.

Some years ago a man asked me to a football game. It was the first of my life, but I accepted. (I would have accepted if he had asked me to a crew race in the Antarctic.) I didn't know much about football, but I did know what time the game started.

It was the Yale–Penn game, and they were playing in Philadelphia. Obviously we would have lunch before the game, and I had visions of some bar and grill where we would eat greasy hamburgers, accompanied by ear-splitting jukebox music. I must have looked doubtful, and so did my Yale man.

"Would it be a terrible imposition if I were to ask you to prepare a picnic luncheon? I hate those greasy...."

I didn't let him finish. "Pick me up at ten," I said and started thinking. A roast chicken? Too banal and also too difficult to eat if you would like to keep your lipstick more or less intact. I had two days to prepare the luncheon, and this is what came out of my hamper on Saturday:

Some stuffed peppers (page 155), which are equally good cold or hot.

Chunks of boiled chicken, skinned, boned, and packed into plastic containers.

Some fairly thick mayonnaise flavored with herbs—to dip or not to dip.

Tiny boiled potatoes, sprinkled with dill, and packed in another container, with a few toothpicks to pick them up.

Cherry tomatoes.

Chunks of mozzarella in another container.

A box of brownies—nothing to rave about, but good and easy to eat.

I had a large basket with enough space for everything. The plates were plastic, but the flatware was silver, the glasses were large goblets, and the salt and pepper were in handsome shakers. The bottle of white wine was enclosed in one of those miraculous bags that keep it chilled for hours, and the coffee was kept hot in an oversized thermos bottle. We had two huge cloth napkins to spread over our laps and lots and lots of paper napkins. (Yale blue, of course). The basket fit neatly between the two seats of his sports car, and we were married three months later.

I have since been to a few more football games, although I still prefer New York's art galleries to a cold wooden bench. But I have prepared luncheons for quite a few, and so here are some tips for picnic lunches.

Cold sliced fillet of beef is very successful, if you don't forget to pack the mustard. Cold pasta salad is not very successful because it is hard to eat. Raw vegetables, such as cauliflower flowerets, carrot sticks, and radishes, are a hit with women but not very popular with men—except possibly for the radishes. Cheeses are good as long as you avoid the runny ones. Don't pack any fish at all—it is to be avoided in any shape or form. Hard-boiled eggs are always enjoyed, particularly if you prepare a small container of salt and pepper mixed together. Bring two corkscrews; one might break in the first bottle. And, most important, don't forget the Towelettes—they are a marvelous invention.

Avoid equipped hampers. They are pretty, cost a fortune, and don't do the job. The napkins are unfailingly inadequate. The plates are never the number you need. There is no container for artificial sweeteners or decaffeinated coffee or other items for special needs. If you like long loaves of bread, the hampers are too small. And if you want to add a large pot of mustard, they won't close.

You are much better off buying a spacious basket and filling it as you go along, starting with the tablecloth and napkins and then adding items as you would set a table: flatware, plates, salt and pepper, a little bottle of salad dressing (prepared by you, I trust), and so on. When you have loaded it, cover it with a nice kitchen towel (very handy to wipe a glass or a plate) and off you go. If it has a broad bottom, the basket will sit comfortably on the backseat of your car, and unless you overload it, it is easy to carry.

Once the picnic is over and you are eager to get home, put everything back, no matter in what order; it all has to go into the dishwasher anyway. If you had one of those glamorous hampers, where everything has its place, you would be struggling trying to put greasy plates, with a little mayonnaise sticking to the edges, back into their elegant leather loops. Not only, but you might have been picnicking where there is no water available to rinse anything and a little red wine might be left in your glasses. Think of what this can do to the pretty calico lining of your fancy hamper! Whereas my basket can take anything. Just put some paper towels in first, and then pile in all your plates, glasses, and condiments. All will be well.

So far I have only spoken about picnics for grown-ups, which is unkind because children enjoy them so much. In fact, I believe that children like them instinctively, whereas adults enjoy them again at a certain age—after they have experienced more sophisticated ways of dining, like "gala dinners" and fancy restaurants.

For children, picnics are wonderful fun. They mean not having to sit still, not having to watch whether their elbows are on the table, not having to be careful that their napkins don't slide to the floor. For mothers, it is a little added work. It means making sandwiches instead of putting cold cuts on a plate, wrapping food instead of placing it simply on the table. But picnics have great advantages.

To be sure, children won't learn table manners when they eat outdoors, but they might learn something about eating. Whereas at home they are only interested in peanut butter and jelly sandwiches, on a picnic they might try cold chicken sandwiches as they are surrounded by green trees and chirping birds. And once they have learned to like foods they have always refused, they might continue to do so. Children, who pretend to despise grown-ups, actually copy them. If they see you eat pears and cheese, they might like to try them instead of insisting on junk food. An aesthetic sense will develop when they study art, but a gastronomic education has to start earlier. A palate is a special thing and can be destroyed in childhood; then it takes decades to learn to enjoy foods again. Some people never learn and miss a lot in life.

AT THE POOL

An obvious, and perfect, place for a party is around a pool—your own or someone else's.

Let's assume that you own a pool and you are giving a luncheon party. (It would be a lot easier in the house or on the terrace, but it's so much more fun by the pool.) If the pool is quite a distance from the house, make sure you have a complete list of everything you need, or you will be running back and forth a lot, and by the time the party comes along you will be exhausted.

If you have a refrigerator near the pool, you have almost no problem. If you don't, be sure you have a lot of ice. I always marvel at the amount of ice I need on a hot day at lunchtime. No matter how large your ice bucket is, you probably will have to go back to the house to refill it at least once.

Near a pool you will, of course, be using plastic glasses and plates. No one wants pieces of broken glass where people walk around barefoot. There's no reason, though, why you shouldn't use your best silver. It doesn't tarnish faster outdoors than indoors, and it adds an elegant note. Also, it is heavy, and you need that weight to hold down plates, napkins, and tablecloth. Take the advice of someone who has swam after plates floating in the pool! For this same reason stay away from paper napkins.

You can't put knives and forks in the goblets, so while they are empty, place some very clean, attractive pebbles in the bottoms. When the time comes to fill them with wine, remove the pebbles. If it's a breezy day, I also place a few pebbles in the breadbasket. Bread alone is usually not heavy enough to keep the basket from flying off. Even on a windless day you get sudden gusts.

Now put on your bathing suit, with something pretty over it. Your guests will start to arrive, and everyone will want to know what that funny little gadget is you have dangling from your wrist. It is black, the size of a pack of cigarettes, and it's a must at any outdoor party. It keeps the bugs away and it really works. If you hold it to your ear, you can hear a very faint sound; apparently it is faint to you, but not to mosquitoes or other bugs. (Don't think that there are no bugs by your pool. I thought so, until the day when I had a guest who was allergic. It was no fun, but that little gadget protects quite a few people.)

Maybe you believe in barbecuing for lunch; I don't. All that charcoal adds to the heat; the breeze invariably blows the smoke in the wrong direction; the flies buzz around the meat while it's cooking; and the smell permeates the hot air. If you want to barbecue, do it in the evening when it's cool.

On the other hand, there are lots of delicious, cool, easy-to-transport dishes that you can bring from the house at the last moment, place on the table, and protect with net covers that open and close like umbrellas.

An ideal dessert is grapes and cheese. Use a rather hard cheese, not one that starts running all over your guests' fingers. (Don't assume that your guests are too civilized to rinse their fingers in your pool. I once thought so too.) Grapes are a very good dessert. They don't require peeling or cutting, and if they are seedless they disappear without leaving a trace. No other dessert is needed, unless you insist on cookies. (Homemade, of course.) And then you'll serve coffee: hot *and* iced. Serve it from large thermos bottles into plastic mugs.

The lovely wife of a United States ambassador to one of the world's most beautiful countries took her job as mistress of an embassy very seriously. She entertained madly, and wisely.

The embassy had a pool, and on good days luncheon was around the pool. The trouble was that she never knew at what time guests would appear, particularly guests from the United States who would love to spend their mornings sightseeing and return to the embassy only when they got tired. Whenever they showed up at the pool, there would be an individual basket waiting for them. It would be standing in the shade with their food and red wine in it, whereas the white wine, in small bottles, was kept cold in an ice bucket.

The food, roasted chicken legs and small fried scaloppine of veal (see page 224), was wrapped in aluminum foil; the glasses were tumblers of silvery plastic. The large napkins that covered the whole basket were cloth.

Some guests wanted to see the city in the moonlight. A dozen or so of those silvery glasses would be placed in a basket and a bottle of fine brandy would be added with maybe a bag of nuts to munch with it. (The advantage of brandy is that you don't have to bother with ice.) Off they would go in a couple of cars to sip their brandy sitting on the steps of the ancient monuments.

But even if you don't have ruins to admire, there might be a hill that overlooks a city, a lake, a river—something beautiful that gets more beautiful at night. You might want to share it with your guests. Whether you take a picnic to the park, have a gathering around your pool, or move on to a local sight for a view, entertaining in this manner does not take a special talent. All it needs is a bit of imagination and a sense of what your guests would enjoy. You don't want to take someone up the steps of an ancient temple in the moonlight if his or her taste runs to discotheques. Nor do you want to inflict a luncheon by the pool on someone who hates to swim, hates water, hates sunshine and, generally hates the outdoors. This is terribly important: don't take it for granted that your guests share your tastes. Check before you plan.

SOME OTHER IDEAS FOR PARTIES

A friend of yours has written a book. You don't inquire about the fate of the manuscript; you know that, if there is good news, you will hear. And then, finally, comes the phone call: "It has been accepted! And by the publisher I most wanted." The voice quivers with emotion, and you immediately live up to the great moment.

"Let's celebrate." You give the new author the number of people you can accommodate, but you leave the choice of guests to the author, in which case you might wind up with people you have never met. But you have to be prepared for anything. You also have to be prepared for some guests arriving early and others coming late. And, most important, you must be available. Can you imagine the arrival of the author's publisher when you are in the kitchen and not there to greet him?

You will, of course, have a buffet. And what you serve depends somewhat on your finances.

You want to make it look festive, so if you have one of those marvelous wooden boards with metal fittings that hold a whole ham (with bone), you are in business. Nothing looks more spectacular than such a ham, held upright by metal straps. You might even get a prosciutto. Part of it will be sliced, and the thin slices will lie languorously on the edge of the wooden board, with a small fork to pick them up. A long, sharp knife will be provided for the adventurous, who will keep slicing.

In the long run such a ham is a good investment because it lasts quite a while. And when there is no meat left on it, the bone makes wonderful soup. But if that is too expensive, there is of course the old stand-by; turkey. Depending on the time of year, it might be a good solution. Between the middle of November and the middle of January, it is definitely a bad idea. People are so tired of the sight of that dear bird that any turkey, no matter how well prepared, only makes them think of the leftovers they have at home.

An unusual chicken salad is always a solution (page 193). So is a vitello tonnato (page 222), but with the price of veal, it becomes a very expensive dish. But there is a trick: use turkey breasts instead of veal. Properly marinated in its sauce, no one will know the difference.

Avoid serving a green salad. If it stands there, for quite awhile with its dressing on it, it will look wilted and depressing. Instead, make a salad of cooked vegetables. String beans (if not in season use long beans, available in all oriental groceries), peas, carrots, cauliflower, and a few potatoes—all cut into neat pieces and dressed with a tasty mustard-flavored mayonnaise—will look good, will taste good, and won't require a knife to eat it.

A rice or pasta salad is good, also not very expensive and not too common, particularly if you use pasta made of buckwheat. It's delicious, also available in oriental groceries, and many people have never seen it before.

A large cheese platter can be made interesting if you experiment with unusual cheeses. With the variety of cheeses now available in this country, you can prepare a fascinating platter.

The same is true of crackers. There seems to be a new cracker on the market every week: white, light brown, dark brown, or black. And they are all good. Avoid the flavored ones, however. They might be satisfactory for children's snacks, but if you serve cheese, you don't want a cracker that is onion flavored or one that adds garlic to a subtle boursin.

You do want a dessert, but you don't want to cope with too many plates. How about a fruitcake? Generously soak it in brandy for that

Shrimps with Peppers and Feta, page 196

touch of something sweet. Remember that for a party like this some people might drop in for a snack on their way to the theater. You don't want them to leave with the taste of cheese on their lips.

As for drinks, you will have everything available you might have at any buffet party. And then, when only the author and just a couple of intimate friends are left, you might open a bottle of champagne. At that point you might also want to serve coffee; no need to serve coffee to people who just drop in to say congratulations.

The kind of party I have just described would also be appropriate for a young actor or actress who has just landed a part, or a friend who has just been made vice-president in charge of something-or-other. It is uncomplicated and friendly. Guests can drop in for ten minutes or stay three hours.

How about remembering your friend's birthday? Or maybe their children's birthdays? How about calling a friend and saying: "Is Emily going to be sixteen next month? I thought so. How about letting me give her birthday party? You are so busy, and I have time. Ask her to invite a few friends, and you add a few grown-ups."

Depending on the hour of the day, you will serve either a birthday cake, which you can buy if you don't know how to make one, and a punch that you can lace with rum so both the youngsters and their parents will enjoy it. A party like that will make both them and you feel that you are part of their lives.

Do you have a yard?. Or a roof, if you live in an apartment building in the city? Not all your friends have summer houses, or early in the season may not have opened theirs. And women like to have brown legs when the time comes to go without hose. Why not ask them over "to get a little sun"? The men can give you a hand planting herbs, and you can serve them drinks and a little cold buffet. Easy and congenial!

Another good reason to entertain is to start the year off right. New Year's Day is a blah day at best, and a bad hangover day at worst.

Everyone has been waiting for midnight, and the start of a new year as if something cosmic were going to happen. And now the new year has come, and all you have is a headache and the thought that in two weeks you will have to pay taxes. But if you ask a few friends to come by between 1 and 3 for a very informal brunch, you have something to take your mind off your problems. And they have something to look forward to.

No one will show up before 1, so you don't have to get up early and you have time for last-minute preparations. Set out large pitchers of bloody Marys and bullshots as your liquid offering. The ideal food to serve is caviar and champagne, but, even if you have asked only one other person, these are so outrageously expensive that most hosts have to rule them out.

Everyone needs something sharp after a long night, so make small anchovy sandwiches (page 129) the night before. If you cover them tightly with wax paper and refrigerate them, they will keep until the next afternoon. The same goes for roquefort sandwiches, unless you want to make a roquefort spread to serve with crackers (page 130). Be sure to have quite a bit of both; some people will arrive at 1:02, and some will trickle in closer to 2. The early ones will continue to munch.

I know a man who prided himself on being a connoisseur of foods. He stated firmly that the first of the year required a piece of herring. If you agree with him, by all means place bite-sized pieces on small squares of pumpernickel and secure them with toothpicks. But don't prepare these tidbits ahead of time; the bread gets soggy.

If it's a very cold day you might not want to limit the food to just cold appetizers. A good strong soup, something like an onion soup or a minestrone, served from one of those large tureens I am so addicted to, adds a reassuring note to the start of a new year. It also helps revive your guests at least for a little while. I have noticed that around 3 they start drooping, no matter how good the conversation started out to be. They start to go home.

Don't take it personally. After all, they have had very little sleep the night before and the next day is a working day.

WHEN THINGS GO WRONG

Though there is no guarantee, well-planned parties are almost certain to be a success. Whether it is a party for friends or what I call a "must" party for your own or your husband's business associates, if you are cool and assured, you can cope with almost anything that comes along. The important thing is not to be jittery. If you can make yourself look forward to it, it will work just as you planned it. However, occasionally even the best organized and carefully prepared party can be ruined by what I call an unforeseen disaster. The following episode is a typical example.

AN UNFORESEEN DISASTER

A charming, vivacious, well-traveled woman from New York was spending some time in Paris. One of Paris' most famous hostesses, well known for her family's vineyards, her spectacular cook, and her stately mansion, gave a luncheon in her honor. Everything was perfect, from the caviar to the champagne, and from the Sèvres dishes to the strawberries grown in the family's hothouses.

The conversation was brilliant and included a remark by the hostess that she would be in New York the following month for a brief stay. Her guest from New York immediately set the date for a luncheon in New York. Then she began to worry. How does one entertain a lady of such perfection?

Her brownstone, though not as grand as the palace in the center of Paris, has great charm; her cook is good, and the butler she hires for such great occasions is better than adequate. And there certainly are enough brilliant people in New York to provide stimulating conversation. But how about the menu? To top the luncheon served in Paris was impossible. To try to duplicate it would be silly and a pale copy at best.

That's when the lady of the brownstone had a brilliant idea: she would serve a New York delicatessen luncheon—a thing totally unknown in France!

An enormous buffet was set with every ethnic specialty, as well as every dish typical of New York. Lox and cream cheese, pastrami, pickled herring, mountains of cole slaw, Virginia ham—a magnificent display of foods that only a New York deli can provide. With this she would serve several brands of beer and a selection of California wines.

When they sat down for lunch, with the sunlight streaming in through the French windows and the butler proudly standing by the buffet, the hostess couldn't help being pleased with herself.

Alas! That pleasure lasted only until the butler placed a plate with a sample of everything in front of the honored guest. She barely looked at all the glory, and announced that she had recently become a vegetarian; she ate almost nothing for lunch and would be pleased if she could have two hard-boiled eggs and nothing else!

At that point the sun disappeared too. The hostess barely had the strength to tell the butler to convey the message to the cook. Two hard-boiled eggs and thirteen minutes to wait, while no one ate and everyone tried to make polite conversation.

The poor cook in the kitchen was so rattled that she forgot even the most basic device. (To make a bed of lettuce, place the eggs on top, and add a few radishes or tiny tomatoes to them—the eggs would at least look acceptable.) But no! The poor woman could only think "two hard-boiled eggs, that's all," and thirteen minutes later the butler returned to the dining room with a platter in his hands, on which lay two eggs, naked and slithering back and forth. Madame ate them without comment, seemingly totally unaware of the crushing blow she had delt the luncheon.

It must have been this display of total calm that shook the hostess out of her gloom. She started to laugh! And, mind you, not a self-conscious giggle. Her handsome head thrown back, she laughed out loud. And, almost immediately, the guests saw the funny side of the situation and joined her. After a moment of astonishment, Madame joined in the general hilarity.

The food disappeared pretty much, and without her help. By the time coffee was served (she did drink that), the conversation was lively, with everyone totally at ease. What could have been a total disaster became a memorable occasion, saved by the hostess' sense off humor.

And this is really the secret: for the hostess to be able to cope when something goes wrong. (I say "hostess" advisedly. For some reason, if a single man entertains and something goes wrong it doesn't seem to matter. Oh! the injustice of it!)

FOOD PREFERENCES
AND ALLERGIES

Changes in eating patterns are one special kind of surprise, but a willing host or hostess sometimes encounters others. I mentioned in an earlier chapter that foods such as chicken livers are inexpensive and quite versatile. Make sure your guests like them before you plan a meal around them, however.

Kidneys are in the same category: one either loves them or hates them. But even I limit myself to veal kidneys, since both beef and lamb are a little beyond me. And I find that squid is another type of food that is served to guests only after checking first. Once, my host at a country luncheon was feeling secure in the knowledge that I had traveled a great deal and would be used to exotic dishes. He served squid; not only that, but his chef prepared it in a special Greek way with cinnamon. The sight of squid makes me quite uncomfortable, but with cinnamon, I come close to despair.

I don't think that anyone noticed. I talked a lot and ate nervously, trying to think of something else. But that luncheon remains in my memory as an act of gastronomic heroism.

There are dishes that your guests couldn't face either, so avoid any uncomfortable situations—for you or them—and ask them first.

There is another problem that hosts and hostesses encounter sometimes: food allergies. Somehow, they didn't seem to be around as much in years past, but now they are very much with us. There are a few that are quite common, like allergies to strawberries or seafood. Guests should warn you that they might get blue or choke, or do something equally discouraging, before you plan the meal.

And then there are some very special allergies. I know a charming, cheerful woman who is allergic to veal. She tells you, which is the only sensible and civilized thing to do. When she told me, I replied, "At today's prices I am allergic to veal too!"

Worst of all, some people who are shy about their allergies and don't confess them until the whatever-it-is is on their plate. They don't realize what an embarrassment they might cause a host and what a damper they might put on a party.

UNEXPECTED GUESTS

Running short on food is a situation that might be quite embarrassing but can easily be avoided, simply by preparing more than you think you will need. Don't worry about leftovers; you can do amazing things with them. But not only might some of your guests suddenly be ravenous, particularly if the food is very good, but also you might find yourself having more guests than you expected. These guests might appear either on very short notice or on no notice at all, and "very short" could be a phone call minutes before the guests are due to arrive. "Would you mind if we brought a couple that has just arrived from Spain? They are charming. We met them last year on our trip, but we didn't expect them this week. We really can't leave them at home."

Of course you say, "Yes, bring them," and try to memorize their names so you can introduce them around. Surely you have enough food for two extra people. You just pray that no one else has unexpected house guests.

Personally I find last-minute extras to be a tremendous imposition, because foreigners, or people from out of town for that matter, might feel lost in a group where they don't know anyone. You don't have time to take them under your wing, and their hosts (or the ones who should be their hosts) are not always thoughtful enough to keep an eye on them. The sight of a couple of lost people, smiling bravely, doesn't add to a party. But first, make sure you can at least feed them properly.

I am, of course, thinking of extra people at a buffet party. No one would have the nerve to bring last-minute additions to a seated dinner. At least I hope not! In any case, have extra food—it almost always works. I say "almost" because even if you have plenty of food as I always have, your extra guest might be a ten-year-old, who can easily eat five lamb chops without taking a breath.

WEATHER CHANGES

There is one possible disaster that takes a lot of careful planning—and praying. The weather!

It is spring, or summer, or early fall, and you plan to eat outdoors—either in the garden, or in the yard, or even on the terrace of your apartment in town. You have, of course, listened to the weather forecast every time it comes on the air. No rain is in sight. Great! Then comes the day of the party. "Our updated weather forecast—possibility of showers toward evening." You cling to the word *possibility*, but even so you better be prepared.

The most important thing is to protect the food. People have a way of finding a dry spot, even if it's in the garage. But a cloudburst on your veal stew and buttered rolls is a tragedy.

Large beach umbrellas are an answer. They are not an ideal answer, mind you, because they usually fit into the center of a round table, which is not ideal for a buffet, and because they are not large enough to protect the whole table. So you have two tables, side by side and as close together as possible. One holds the meat or fish or both, and the other has the breads and salads. If it then turns out that you didn't need them because the showers don't materialize, all the better. But at least you won't be scanning the sky like an air-raid warden until the danger is past.

If you don't care how much the party costs, you can rent a tent. I find them to be only a last resort. If the weather turns cold, they don't protect you; if it's hot and humid, all the humidity seems to gather under that tent. And—hot or cold—they create a gloomy light which makes everyone look miserable. (Which is, of course, what everybody is.)

Once the food is safe, there is something almost cheerful about a group of people scurrying in from the sudden rain. They will sit on the floor, perch on the arms of chairs, invade your bedroom, and have a wonderful time devouring your marvelous food which, thanks to your talent for organizing a party, has not gotten soggy.

There is another weather hazzard: heat!

It hit me a couple of weeks ago. We had had splendid weather: not too hot and delightfully dry. I had planned a Sunday lunch for what started to be a group of about twenty and grew to forty-seven. There would be no problem. A few guests would want to stay indoors, but most of them would want to be outdoors in what my husband calls "God's green air."

Sunday came and with it, a temperature in the high nineties and a humidity that would have made orchids ecstatic. The trouble was that I hadn't invited any orchids, and to see one's friends wilt is a sad sight indeed.

The first thing I did was pull all the drapes and close all the doors and windows. We have a modest amount of air conditioning in our little house in the country—barely adequate when we are just the two of us, and totally inadequate for forty-seven. I turned it on anyway, full blast, and started phoning a few friends who have electric fans. "Bring them, please, and tell your husband to leave his tie and coat at home." They brought the fans, bless them, but they bravely wore their ties.

I set the food in the coolest place in the house, not only to keep it perky (it was all cold, of course) but also to make our guests feel that things weren't too bad and that maybe the outdoors were endurable. Wherever there was a patch of shade, I set up little tables, complete with umbrellas and citronella candles, and with buckets full of ice holding bottles of white wine. Believe it or not, most people chose the outdoors and survived, seemingly happily. (I was in the pool before the last car left our driveway.)

DIFFICULT GUESTS

People come in all shapes and sizes, especially the difficult ones. And, as they probably don't know that they are difficult, they don't warn you.

First, there are those who, at the end of a good, long dinner, can't tear themselves away. You also have been having a good time, but are aware that you have to clean up, go to bed, and then get up early the next morning. You feel like saying, "I have to get up at seven. Do you mind going home?" but of course you can't. So make a note of whom they are and remember to ask them for lunch next time.

Then there are the kind who are barely annoying, and not outright disastrous. I had recently encountered such a person. We were giving a dinner party in the country, and a few hours before the guests were due to arrive, one of them called to say that her father had suddenly descended on them. Could they bring him? Could I say no?

I expected a gentle, quiet old gentleman. He wasn't. He was barely elderly and not a bit gentle. He didn't thank us for letting him join us at such short notice; he behaved as if it were an honor for us. It was not a very large party and I tried to be polite by including him in the conversation. That was a mistake. Not only did he contradict everybody, he also interrupted. A friend tried to help me by telling a funny story. In the middle of it, "Father" said, "That's a very old story. Besides, you are not telling it correctly." Whereupon he took over.

I rushed drinks and appetizers and started dinner earlier than I had planned. It was not supposed to be a very large party, so I had splurged on two whole filets: one rare, one well done. To make quite sure that no one would get the wrong one, I had placed a small red flag in the rare one and had explained the reason. "Father" helped himself to two hefty slices and sat down in the most comfortable place. The buffet was in one room and small tables for four each were set up in the next room, with the exception of one table that was set for five. He ignored it. At that point I was pretty angry, and—yes—I made him sit where I had placed him, pleading with my eyes for understanding from his dinner companions.

The next time I looked at him he was handing his plate to the waitress, the two slices of splendid meat untouched. "Far too rare for me," he explained. It gave me a little pleasure to think that he must have gone home hungry. Had I known what to expect, I might have found the courage to tell his daughter that I was sorry, but we didn't have an extra chair, or knife or fork. Short of doing that, I would have made it impossible for him to take part in the conversation. Finally, I would have been firm about helping him at the buffet— even over his protests.

The trouble is that one frequently doesn't know what to expect—at least not the first time. If you did, you probably wouldn't invite such people; except, of course, that even if you know, you sometimes can't avoid it.

Suppose you have a long-time woman friend. You have gone to college together and have remained very close. Then she marries a bore, or someone who drinks too much and can't handle it. What do you do? Cut her out of your life? Or limit your contact to occasional luncheons for the two of you? Invent excuses or pretend that he doesn't exist? None of the above; meaning, you put up with him.

Whether his problem is that he is a bore or that he can't handle his liquor (frequently the two go together), you invite the couple only with people you know well and, if possible, who know them well. Even so, keep the cocktail hour to a minimum. I have found it helpful to ask everybody for 7:30 and "them" for 8. But you have to do it so no one is aware of it. You also try to steer him away from hard liquor toward wine or sherry. This might be impossible; he probably knows what he wants to drink and insists on it.

You can't deprive your other guests of drinking wine with their meal. The only thing you can do to prevent "him" from drinking too much is to use smaller glasses. Normally I dislike them and find them depressing, but if it discourages the man from drinking too much it's worth it.

But your troubles aren't over with dinner; he might want an after-dinner drink. Normally I ask my guests if they want one, and I find that most people don't, particularly if it's a weekday evening and they have to go to work the next day. But I always have a tray with drinks in the living room—except when I have that difficult guest! If drinks are within reach, he will help himself to one even if you don't offer it to him. But if there are no bottles around, he might feel self-conscious about asking.

No matter what you do, you won't enjoy the evening and neither will his wife. Be grateful that you are not married to him. But you do want to bring the evening to an early end, and unfortunately you can't get rid of him alone.

Once in my life I had to take extreme measures. Such a guest had gotten cantankerous and his poor wife was fidgeting. I got up and said, "We are such old friends that I know you will understand. I have a very early breakfast meeting tomorrow. Please forgive me." They left, and I still wince when I think of it. I apologized to the other guests the next day.

Difficult houseguests are much more of a problem. You have them on your hands until Sunday night (if not until Monday morning!), and no one can deliver you of them.

I could, of course, tell you not to invite people for a weekend if you don't know them well enough to be sure that they would be congenial. But you might have known someone for years; lunched, dined, and gone to exercise class with them. In your own home, and for more than a few hours, they could turn out to be different people.

I had asked Sylvia to spend a weekend with us in the country. Her husband had recently left her, and she seemed lost and vulnerable. I had known her for quite awhile, and I know that she is a perfectionist and used to living in a grand style, so I had warned her that our house in the country was no marble palace and that all we had in the way of servants was a maid who came in during the week when we weren't there to do the cleaning.

When I saw Sylvia's luggage, I felt a little shudder. Heavens. Three large bags! How long was she planning to stay? I took her to the guest room, which is downstairs from the rest of the house and has privacy but not much space. It is, however, a pretty room; black and white, with a black and white bathroom connected to it. It also holds a very good early American chest of drawers.

Not a peep out of her. (She could have said "pretty." She didn't.) "I'll let you get settled, my dear. If you need something, holler. And when you are ready come down to the pool, it's down there." I pointed toward the window and through a forest of hollyhocks about which we are terribly proud. She didn't look up. "I don't swim," she said, adding, "at least not in a pool."

It was a hot day. "Well, I do," I said as gently as I could, "but I'll be back in half an hour or so and we will have drinks."

As I started going up the stairs she called me back. "I have my own pillow with me. Where do I put yours?"

"Pile them on the other bed," I responded without turning back.

I cooled down in the pool, but I later realized that I couldn't stay there. As I got out, the phone rang. It was Roberto, a charming friend of ours. He was alone, his wife was in Europe for the summer, and he was hot. Could he come out? Ah, as if someone had thrown me a lifeline! I explained that the guest room was occupied, but there was a bed in the study, if he didn't mind. He didn't let me finish: "Be there in an hour," he said and hung up.

I told my husband, who seemed as relieved as I was. Sylvia didn't comment. I had an excuse to leave Sylvia to my husband while I made the bed in the study. Our additional guest arrived even before the hour was up.

"You have a pool? How marvelous. Can we have a swim? Can we take drinks down there with us?" While he was talking, he was shedding garments and picking them up. He ran upstairs to deposit his clothes and came back wearing his bathing trunks. Roberto then picked up a couple of bottles, handed the astonished Sylvia the ice bucket to carry, gave me some plastic glasses, and admired the hollyhocks: "They look like Fragonard." In other words, he breathed life into the dismal picture that we were before his arrival.

And Sylvia did indeed come to life. She draped herself over a chaise by the pool and started talking. Incessantly! Until Roberto threatened to splash her and her chiffon caftan with water: "Let someone else talk too," he told her. As hostess, I couldn't say that.

Then came the time to get dinner. Roberto handed Sylvia a piece of Parmesan cheese to grate, while he and I were to make tagliatelle. She objected because she had to get dressed for dinner. "Okay," he said, "then you will grate it after you have dressed." She grated—complaining and assuring us that she was ruining her hands, but she grated! My husband and I were having a ball. And dinner was fun, as we got into Roberto's spirit. Sylvia had no choice: either join us or go to bed. She joined.

The next morning she appeared, wearing white silk pants and an elaborate silk shirt (both made to order in Paris, we were told). She hadn't been able to sleep all night because her room was too hot.

"And I thought I heard you snore," said Roberto with a face as innocent as a cherub's.

After a substantial breakfast, which she only ate because she had no appetite, she wandered out on the terrace for a breath of air, and sat on a chair that was still covered with morning dew. In a second, she was back inside, shaken as if a tarantula had bitten her. She was wet! This required a change of costume. But it also required that she tell everyone who came later for an informal luncheon about the terrible thing that had happened to her.

Roberto was having a great time; I was not. After all, she wasn't *his* guest. But he finally took pity on me.

"I am going to tell her that you plan to stay out here for a couple of days and that I will give her a lift into town before evening. That will give you a little rest."

He did, she accepted, and they left—he with a big grin, she with a frown; my husband and I sighing with relief.

To avoid such a house guest is impossible because you never know how a person will behave. How to cope, once you are stricken with one, is by having someone around who doesn't have to take such a person seriously and knows how to make a joke of it.

And then there are the clumsy guests. I have a large blue and white rug in the living room; that's my mistake. Knowing what a beating the rug takes, I should have chosen darker colors. But there it is and I love it. Unfortunately it seems to attract the clumsy guest.

One time, people had barely sat down at the small tables before a large glass of red wine went flying, landing on the rug. Fortunately I had a butler that night who knew what to do. He poured a bottle of soda water over the wine and started mopping it up, while the clumsy guest stood there saying, "You will of course send me the bill from the cleaner."

"Never mind the bill: just help us mop up the mess," I said, handing him a roll of paper towels. I said it laughingly, of course, and the whole thing was over in minutes.

When something precious gets broken, the situation requires a bit of self-control. This happened at a seated dinner for ten. The guest of honor was a delightful woman of whom I am deeply fond. Her only shortcoming is that she is indeed clumsy.

Though I was aware of it, I was using some priceless antique wine glasses. I used to own a dozen of them, but now only nine are left. At a dinner for ten, I use one similar glass that doesn't quite match, and that glass will probably be with me forever—it's the nine good ones that are an endangered species. That night one of them lost its life, at the hand of the guest of honor.

She was crestfallen. Knowing that she is clumsy, she is also very self-conscious. My heart went out to her. "What difference does it make?" I said. "If I still had a dozen, it might be different but whether I have nine or eight is totally immaterial. Actually eight is a better number," and I quickly brought out another glass, picking up the pieces of the broken one with as little fuss as possible.

The next day four Baccarat glasses arrived, with a rose tied to them and a note, "To a great hostess." The accolade was not really deserved, but I have learned to make light of small disasters. If someone ruins your tablecloth, it really makes no sense to allow it to ruin your party too.

Only once did I almost lose my cool. A female dinner guest had insisted on helping soak the soiled dishes in the kitchen sink. It was a party at which I had no help, and she had a system! That she had alright. She left the water running. By the time we noticed it, the water was seeping from the kitchen into the dining room. We all mopped it up with sponges, rags, paper towels, and whatever we could get hold of. We were ankle deep in suds, but she wasn't. She just stood there, shaking her head. I didn't quite tell her what I thought of her performance, but she is off my guest list.

And there are the "nuisance guests." They are simply difficult by nature, and one has to learn to cope with them.

A typical example are the attention-seekers. They tell you endless tales about a trip to France, where everybody else had been too, and their story has no particular interest except that they mispronounce some of the names.

If dinner is ready and he or she won't stop talking, you might yell: "Will the senator yield? Dinner is ready," which will at least show that you have been to Washington. If that particular attention-seeker is holding forth at the dinner table and won't let go, be ready to strike the moment there is a brief pause. (Everyone has to stop for breath) then say to another guest: "Haven't you told me that you have found a delightful new hotel in Avignon?" or "Is that traffic in Monte Carlo so bad that you can't cross the street?" Ask anything to make the virulent talker realize that he isn't the only person in the room who travels. Just have a remark ready, and be quick.

There is also the opposite of the long-distance talker and that is the silent guest. He or she just sits there, maybe smiling a little now and then, but won't say a word. It's up to you to draw him or her into the conversation.

If you know beforehand that you will have this problem, find out about his or her hobby; most everyone has one. Then ask: "Where are you playing tennis these days?" or "I know I should remember, but how big was that bass you caught off Cuttyhunk?" The latter is a dangerous question. The silent guest might turn into a relentless talker, complete with photos that he "just happened to have" in his wallet. Never mind. Anything is better than that silent presence.

At the end of one of these parties, or weekends, ask yourself if it's worth putting up with their shortcomings. Do they have other charms and do you want to ask them again? Unless it is for business reasons or the husband of an old friend, give yourself an answer in the negative, and don't ask them again. At least not for awhile.

SOME ENTERTAINING
QUESTIONS AND ANSWERS

I am frequently asked my advice on matters of entertaining, especially on those subjects usually ignored by other party books—maybe because they are taken for granted or maybe authors think that you should make your own mistakes and learn from your own experiences. Why, if a little hint can be so useful?

What pots and pans do you recommend having? Which ones come in the handiest, without loading up the kitchen with unnecessary gadgets?

There are several implements and gadgets—large and small—that make life easier for the host or hostess, especially those who can't count on help from others.

Although pots and pans are such a personal thing, we all know that heavy skillets—either cast iron or heavy aluminum—are best for frying and sautéeing. I have inherited a whole batch of iron skillets, but I've never even used the largest one because I simply can't lift it, not even when it's empty. (My grandparents must have had hefty cooks.) But if you are strong enough, a large cast-iron skillet is what you should use. The more space food has to sauté in, the better. If you can't handle a large skillet, sauté several pieces of meat or fowl in batches.

Good knives are a must in a well-equipped kitchen, but they too are very personal. A chopping knife should have a blade that is wide enough to prevent your knuckles from hitting the chopping board, but since knuckles also vary in size, you will have to judge what size knife will fit your hand. Or you might use one of those moon-shaped choppers with a wooden handle on each end. They not only chop well, they are also good for your figure because they force you to do a little dance with your hips.

As for paring knives, I like a very thin, very small blade. You might prefer a longer version, however. And a slicing knife has only to be sharp.

A kitchen tool I never want to be without is a pair of tongs, available in any hardware store. With these you can turn whatever you are frying or roasting or sautéing—much preferable to stabbing the food with a fork. Every time I see someone stick a fork into a piece of meat, I whimper because the precious juices are being lost. The same goes for a piece of chicken you are broiling.

I have small spatulas, although others prefer longer ones. And I like to have several of them, not only because one might be in the dish-washer when I most need it, but also because I use two spatulas to turn or lift a roast. Never a fork! Remember those juices?

A small gadget that some people might find useful is an apple corer. It cores and cuts apples into sections and can also be used for radishes, provided they are quite large.

I go crazy in housewares departments and stores the way some other women become excited about a sale of pantyhose. There is a particularly good store in San Francisco (Williams-Sonoma), where I located a cloth parsley drier that keeps the herb crisp for days, just as the larger bag keeps your salad crisp. That is also where I found a small potato peeler with a small hook on one side to remove the eyes from potatoes.

Solid functional chopping boards are also important. Forget the flimsy ones with the cute sayings; you need boards for chopping vegetables, but also for slicing meats. And if you have a solid butcher block type, you can even bring it to the table and serve a ham or roast beef directly from it (with juices separate in a gravy boat). There is talk about the unsanitary nature of such wooden chopping boards, however, because the wood absorbs some of the meat or fish juices. Wipe yours off carefully, or use a plastic chopping board. I don't like them as much, but now I use the plastic board for cutting up raw fish or fowl and the wooden board for all other uses. And I use a good detergent for both, plus a strong rinsing with warm water afterwards.

Another important item in the kitchen is a colander. You certainly have a large one for your pasta or your vegetables. Mine is a gleaming copper beauty. It has one shortcoming though: the holes are meant for pasta. If I try to drain rice in it the grains either go right through the holes or, if I am lucky, they get stuck in them. So you need another one, best made of steel mesh, that will hold the rice.

I have a couple of recipes that call for passing hard-cooked eggs through a sieve. The holes of your colander are too big and the mesh of your tea strainer are too small. In other words: you need two colanders and two sieves—at least! And remember, the sieves don't last forever. Examine the edges on your elderly sieves carefully; when the wires start to break, throw them out lest you get little pieces of wire into your food.

I can't cook! Is there any hope for me?

Yes, you can cook. This feeling is more a state of mind than a lack of talent, and it can be overcome. Believe me, I know! I was not quite eighteen years old when I found myself married to a man who had to entertain quite frequently and quite formally. And I barely knew how to bring water to a boil. I learned fast, probably because I began to enjoy it. And this is the important point.

The recipes I've included in this book are mostly very simple. They are meant for those people who look at their pots and pans and feel lost.

My advice is that you try by starting with simple things. Follow the instructions, and you will have no problems. And stay away from so-called short-cuts; they usually are more trouble than they are worth. For example, I have tried some of those frozen vegetables that come in a pouch. I discovered that boiling the pouch, without allowing it to disappear into the boiling water, fishing it out when it is time, and finally cutting it to get at the contents without seeing them run all over the kitchen table is far more complicated and requires more skill than some simple recipe that is more delicious and will also give you that wonderful feeling of accomplishment.

Can you give me some advice on selecting and buying cheese? It all seems so confusing.

It does seem that many people, upon entering a cheese store, are totally confused. "They all look more or less alike," complains a friend of mine. "How does one know what they taste like?"

I used to feel that a salesperson in a good cheese store should be able to guide you, but having repeatedly found that not to be so, I am suggesting that you learn about cheese yourself.

There seems to be a cockeyed rule that soft cheeses (the types that spread) are elegant and semisoft or hard cheeses aren't. So, brie and boursin are everywhere. They are perfectly respectable cheeses—very rich and caloric—but they get a little monotonous, especially if you go to three dinners in one week and encounter three bries and three boursins.

I can understand that you would eat camembert only in the privacy of your home. It's a delicious cheese, but somewhat too self-asserting. More or less the same can be said about gorgonzola, that wonderful green and white marbled cheese from northern Italy. If you have never experienced it, try it as least once, particularly in the fall with fresh walnuts.

If you are not fond of sharp cheeses, what about a Lorraine? Or a Bel Paese, also from Italy. They are gentle and yet aromatic. The latter is wrapped in tinfoil with a round label in the middle. Careful! One Bel Paese has the two Americas on the label, the other a picture of the boot that is Italy. The former is made in this country, the latter is imported. They are both good but slightly different, the Italian version being a little richer.

We all know swiss cheese and we all love it, though secretly. Somehow that poor cheese has acquired the reputation of being associated with the call, "One ham and swiss on rye; one coffee and cream," to be handed to the "go-for" who waits at the counter of a deli at lunchtime.

How unjust! And how unjust that only foreigners seem to appreciate munster, whereas Americans, who grew up with it, think little of it. Could it be that both these excellent cheeses have had their reputation ruined by being sliced, individually wrapped, and therefore not fit to be placed on a cheese platter. Look around. Heaven be praised, both can still be bought in lusty huge chunks to compete with all sorts of cheeses with names that are hard to pronounce.

There are two cheeses, unlike any others, I am especially fond of: one Greek, one Italian. The first is, of course, feta. It is quite sharp and not to be eaten in large quantities, but crumble it and sprinkle it over a good salad, season the salad with good olive oil, and you will have a feast. (And I don't usually go in for cheese salad dressings!) Or make an omelette stuffed with feta and allow the cheese to melt slightly. Great!

The other cheese is fontina. It really has that nutty flavor one hears so much about and finds so rarely. The only problem is that it is almost impossible to stop eating it once one has started. It is great with fruit and is, in my opinion, the only cheese that lends itself to be melted over veal, chicken, or beef. (Sorry, swiss, I like you but not hot.)

Be careful when you buy fontina; there are two kinds. One has a brownish rind and comes from Italy, the other has a red rind and comes from Denmark. They have really very little in common. The Scandinavian variety is perfectly respectable, but it doesn't come near a real fontina. Also, it doesn't melt properly.

And then there is Parmesan—The king of all cheeses! You have eaten it grated, more or less pure, or more or less mixed with lesser cheeses. But you have not had it in chunks, to nibble with nuts, fruit, or simply a good crusty bread. If you have just had a raise, invest in a hunk of Parmesan. Place it in the center of your cheese platter, add a knife with a sharp point (it should not be sliced, but broken into chunks), and you will be known as "that divine host or hostess who serves Parmesan in chunks." It has one shortcoming: Parmesan is outrageously expensive, but it's worth it.

There are about 1,000 known cheeses on this planet. I only know about 300, but even that makes it impossible to mention all of them. There are the Edams and the Goudas and a whole series of cheddars. They are all good and have their followings. The only prejudice I have is against cheeses that aren't genuine. The "cheese foods," and—equally to be avoided—the cheeses flavored with something that isn't their own flavor.

If I want to eat nuts with my cheese I am perfectly capable to do so, and if I want pimiento with my cheese I know what to do about it. But I don't want a manufacturer of prepared cheeses to force them on me.

Sounds logical? Maybe only to a cheese lover such as I. I remember a doctor once telling me that I should reduce my intake of cheese, whereupon I burst into tears!

I'm never sure if I'm serving the right wine. What is proper?

You know the rules, of course. Red wines are served with red meats; white wines with fowl, fish, and maybe veal. But don't stick to the rules too sternly. If some of your guests are enjoying a light Muscadet or a Soave before dinner and would like to continue with it, don't make them feel like outcasts because your main course calls for a red wine. After all, people have a right to their wine tastes. I have been guilty of drinking a white wine that I am particularly fond of, even though the dish called for a red.

In my opinion there are only two no-nos. They are never to serve a sweet wine with dinner (except if you are serving pâté de foie gras) and never to serve the so-called wine that goes with everything. There is no such wine. If it "goes with everything," it really goes with nothing.

Also, we have been taught since childhood that white wines should be chilled and red wines served at room temperature. And so they should be. But that doesn't mean that the whites should be frozen to the point that they almost lose their flavor. And when we say "room temperature," we didn't think of 80-degree steamheat. Particularly for a young red—such as a Beaujolais or a young Chianti— cellar temperature would be more appropriate.

And then there is the rule about opening a bottle beforehand. A good old red should be allowed some time to breathe. (It hasn't been breathing for so many years.) But if you open a young wine and let it stand for a few hours, nothing good will happen to it. (I am not talking about those rare great reds of noble vintage. They should not be allowed to breathe and only true wine drinkers should serve, or drink them.)

And finally, white wines should be drunk young. Sturdy white Burgundies can stand a little more age, but gentle Soaves or Pinots should really not be older than about three years. Once you have opened them, drink them. I find that a good white wine, properly re-corked will stand two to three days in the refrigerator but not more. Some even balk at that length of time.

I don't have many tablecloths and napkins, and what I have doesn't seem to fit together well. What is important in setting the table?

The table should be pretty. I am not suggesting you set out a precious lace cloth over pure silk satin. Sure, that would be beautiful and, if you have them, by all means use them. But you can set an attractive table with much simpler things as well. Like tablecloths that you can make yourself, if you have the time, or can buy for very little in any department store, particularly if you go during their January white sales.

I love a white tablecloth and, except for special occasions such as Thanksgiving or Christmas (when I use a bright red one), I always use white. In summer, for outdoor parties, however, it is a different matter; I go wild with color.

And I love colored napkins. Picture this: an immaculate tablecloth and orchid napkins loosely tied with the narrowest pale blue ribbon. Be careful though. Don't use dishes with a loud pattern; the dishes should also be white or any solid color.

And don't feel bad if, after you have gone through all that trouble, no one remarks on your lovely table. Remember that some people feel it is below their dignity to admire someone else's taste; and there are, of course, other people who don't notice. But make no mistake. A pretty table sets the mood for a party.

And then when you least expect it, you find that someone has noticed. I had done one such table setting at Christmastime: a white cloth and bright red napkins tied with a tiny green ribbon. No one said anything, but I didn't care. I enjoyed it. But a few days later, one of the guests called me. "Where did you get that tiny ribbon?" Her husband had noticed and told her, "Some table that was!"

And, if you have a very beautiful table, either antique wood or with a heavy glass top, you might not want to use any cloth at all. A famous antique dealer in New York said, "I would rather see a well-polished elegant wooden top than any tablecloth, no matter how elaborate." He might be right.

Some hostesses don't like placemats because they have to be washed and ironed and are more trouble than just one cloth. This is sometimes true, but there are other alternatives. I have mentioned earlier in the book that for informal meals, rattan or bamboo mats are very acceptable. And, if money is no problem, there are some absolutely stunning Lucite mats. Some look like crystal and cost a fortune, and some are white and look like marble. They require only a soft, damp cloth to be kept pristine. The napkins should be of cloth, no matter what the mats are made of.

A friend of mine has one of the most dramatically beautiful tables I know. The top is one enormous, thick slab of glass. She sometimes uses neither cloth nor mats. With the flames of candles reflecting on it, the table is magic. She only places an invisible soft flannel pad under each plate to protect the glass and keep the plate from making a clatter.

Flowers are a beautiful centerpiece but they are so expensive. What other possibilities are there?

You can make almost anything the attraction of your table. Maybe you own something unusual and particularly beautiful. Feature it. A precious figurine? A porcelain bird? A small tureen that you can fill with simple flowers and place the lid against it?

I own some really beautiful porcelain. It is pure white with some intricate open-work borders. Some of it is eighteenth century and all of it is precious. And all of it I use. The glow of elegance that these dishes give to even the simplest dinner is worth any risk of breakage.

Actually something "special" doesn't have to be an object. You might have access to something special like bread, either baked by you or bought from a special baker not many people know about. Make it the center of your party.

Picture this: you have two or three loaves of spectacular bread. If it has been around for a day or so, place it briefly in a 300-degree oven. Then put the loaves in the center of your table. If you intend to cut them, place a wooden board under them and a large knife beside them. If you intend to tear them apart, you don't need anything except a good vacuum cleaner the next morning.

Remember that bread freezes well. When you take it out of the freezer, place it immediately into a hot oven, without letting it defrost first. When you break it it will crackle, which is still one of the most beautiful sounds in gastronomy, and the perfume of fresh bread will fill the air.

The bread will be your table decoration, and I can't think of a more attractive or appetizing one. (Not for a very formal party, of course.)

I remember one such occasion: I was giving a dinner in the country. Among my guests was a man we all made gentle fun of. It was gentle because he was really a very nice man; he was just slightly stuffy and formal. He was the type who not only kisses your hand but also bows from the waist when he does so. He entered the dining room and there was that gigantic bread practically gleaming on the white tablecloth. "How chic!" he exclaimed. It had never occurred to anyone else that bread could be "chic" but that is how it has remained in our vocabulary.

I often use candles on my table. Is there anything special I should know?

Ever since I was a child I was taught that candles should always look as if they had been lit before. In other words, if you light them in the presence of your guests, the wick should be black, not white. New candles are supposed to be tacky, as if you were wearing a dress that still has the price tag on.

It has become such a habit with me to light the candles that I automatically do it as I insert fresh ones in the candlesticks. I blow them out immediately. This might sound a little silly, but many things that are gracious are also silly.

My apartment doesn't lend itself to formal dinners and my husband doesn't like cocktail parties. Is there something in between?

A lot of people seem to have that problem. The result is a rather new way of entertaining—it is neither a dinner nor a cocktail party. You are invited from 6 to 9 or from 7 to 10. The food, mostly cold, is placed on a table in a corner or on a sideboard. It might be hidden by a screen but that is not necessary.

When most of the guests have arrived you set up small tables that will hold a plate, a knife and fork, and a wine glass, which each guest picks up from the buffet. The guests help themselves and sit at one of the small tables. The wine is poured at the buffet, so that no harrassed host has to wind his way through the maze to pour the wine. The knife and a fork are wrapped in a napkin, which makes it easy to pick up.

There will always be someone who, after having picked up all the implements and having heaped the food on his plate, will stand around near the buffet making it impossible for others to help themselves. Be ruthless! Tell the guest that there are small tables waiting and that he is in the way of other guests.

This kind of party has all sorts of advantages. You don't really *have* to serve a dessert. Cookies or Italian macaroons will do, as will brownies—anything that doesn't require extra plates or flatware.

People will go home by 10 P.M. and not keep you up till all hours; finally, you don't really *have* to serve coffee. If you feel brave, by all means do so. But I find coffee to be a terrible nuisance. Most like it hot but some like it decaffeinated. Some like sugar, some artificial sweeteners, some like cream or milk, and some like nothing. No matter what, you will have a lot of small cups to wash. And if your household is anything like mine, one or two of those tiny spoons will wind up in the garbage never to be found again.

But the small effort of setting up little tables is well worth it. It prevents people from saying that you have thrown just another cocktail party.

Is there anything you particularly dislike?

Yes, I am allergic to cute food. I can't stand hard-cooked eggs that have been made to look like chicks or cheeses that have been tortured to be like mushrooms. Stuffed eggs should look like eggs and cheeses like cheeses. There is a subtle line between imagination and bad taste, and advise all wise folk to stay on the side of imagination.

When you give a party, what is especially important to you?

I am manical about two subjects. The first is that foods that are meant to be hot should be eaten hot, or at least as hot as possible. Have you ever prepared a chicken à la king, only to see it get that glazed look, as the sauce congeals?

The other is that noodles should be avoided on a buffet table. Whether you call them noodles or tagliatelle, they are not supposed to be standing there idly. They should be cooked just right, tossed with either butter and cheese or a sauce, and eaten! Why destroy their charm by placing them on a buffet to wait patiently for guests to help themselves, while they get cold and stick to one another? No matter how carefully they have been prepared, they become a gooey mess.

SUGGESTED
SEASONAL MENUS

T he basis of successful entertaining is a well-balanced menu. You don't want sauce following sauce, or one spicy dish after another. But that isn't all. Meals should be geared to the seasons. Not only because all ingredients are best when they are in season, but also because spring and summer meals should be light, and heavier dishes should be reserved for cold seasons. An unforgettable summer luncheon comes to mind: it was 90° in the shade and the main course on the buffet was hot stuffed peppers in a thick tomato sauce. The guests left early—sweaty and angry. Don't do that to your guests.

Asterisks denote recipes that are included in this book; adjust the quantities as you need.

A SPRING LUNCHEON

Fresh Asparagus Vinaigrette
Tuna or Salmon Layered Mousse*
Chèvre with Fresh Strawberries

This is an ideal meal when you want to be outdoors and not standing by a hot stove.

Cook the asparagus al dente, then cover it with your favorite vinaigrette sauce. Hard cook an egg and press it through a sieve, and sprinkle the egg over the tips of the asparagus. Be sure to cover only the tips; some people like to pick asparagus up with their fingers, which becomes a problem if the stems are covered with bits of egg. You might want to serve the asparagus on individual plates. They may be prepared in the morning, since they are served cold.

The tuna (or salmon) mousse may be prepared the evening before. If it looks too frozen, unmold it an hour before lunch and place it only briefly back in the refrigerator before serving.

Serve some really good, lusty bread with your goat cheese—the kind of bread that makes you feel that you would like to break it apart rather than cutting it.

Good strong coffee, decaffeinated or not, belongs at the conclusion.

The choice of wine presents a little problem. The rule is to serve a white wine with fish, whereas the goat cheese definitely calls for a red. That is easily solved. Tuna is rich enough not to be over-powered by a light red. I would suggest a young Beaujolais or an equally young Chianti. (Beaujolais has a short lifespan; Chianti on the other hand ages beautifully but it also gets heavier with age, and a fine old Chianti would be totally unsuitable with the tuna mousse.) Either wine should be served cool. Place it in the refrigerator for half an hour before serving.

A SPRING DINNER

Scallops and Grapefruit Salad*
Veal Stew with Fresh Peas*
Dressed Green Salad, Sprinkled with Chives
Ricotta Pudding with Chocolate*

If you belong to the lucky people who have their own yard and grow their own peas, pick them when they are small and tender. The age and size of the peas make a big difference in the taste of this stew.

If you have access to a country vegetable stand, try to get the owner to pick some tiny peas for you. It took me awhile to get friendly enough with our vegetable purveyor, but now I can get small peas, tiny green beans, and even baby zucchini (no longer than 4 inches). I am not sure the owner understands why I don't wait until they get big and sassy, but he sells them to me anyway.

The same goes for the salad. If you can get lettuce with tiny leaves, wait until the last moment to pour the dressing over it. The leaves are so tender that the vinegar "cooks" them if they stand around. Chop the chives ahead of time and sprinkle them over the salad at the last moment.

If the weather has turned really warm, give your guests a choice between hot and iced coffee.

A dry white wine—not too fruity lest it overwhelm the scallops—is needed with this meal. A white from Tuscany, or a delicious Pinot Bianco (also called Pomino)—a recent arrival from Northern Italy—would be perfect.

A SUMMER LUNCHEON

Cold Consommé with a Dash of Sherry
Curried Shrimp and Rice Salad*
Mixed Green Salad
Lemon Sherbet with a Dash of Rum

The shrimp and rice salad may be prepared the evening before and refrigerated; just don't add the mayonnaise until serving time. Then remove the salad from the refrigerator a couple of hours before lunch, add the mayonnaise at the last minute, toss, and serve. Pick and wash the greens the night before and place them in a canvas bag in the refrigerator overnight. Prepare your dressing the night before also and pour it into a bottle or a jar with a tight-fitting lid; you want to be able to shake it well before pouring it over the salad.

Serve the sherbet in individual little bowls and pass the rum in its original bottle for every guest to serve him or herself. (I make a point of serving the rum in its bottle because people want to see what rum they are getting.)

I usually feel that bread should be very good and interesting, not just "any sort of bread." In this case it matters little; with the rice, people will hardly touch it. Serve espresso coffee if your guests like it. On a hot day some might like ice tea. Be prepared.

What wine to serve with this luncheon? You have a dash of sherry in the consommé and a dash of rum in the sherbet. If you can afford it, a very dry (brut) Champagne would be ideal.

You don't have to go to the very great and very expensive brands, and a vintage Champagne to boot, but a nonvintage of a lesser known brand is really not much more expensive than a good still wine. And Champagne adds immensely to a meal, particularly at lunch time. (Keep in mind that Champagne is a heavy drink. I remember a very famous French restaurateur—a legend in New York—who said that Champagne should never be drunk after 4 P.M. I have frequently ignored his advice and have sometimes regretted it.)

If you feel that Champagne is either too expensive or too showy, a good very dry white Côte du Rhône, a Macon Blanc, or a Pinot Bianco would be fine.

Note: This menu brings to mind an incident that happened when I was giving a party for a rather large group. I had help for serving. To my dismay a young woman who didn't have much experience appeared with a pitcher into which she had poured the rum. This would have been a mistake at any rate, no matter how pretty the pitcher. In this particular case, it was worse. I had used that pitcher to water my indoor plants and I had added some fertilizer to the water! I usually rinsed it well, so no one tasted anything and no guests got sick, but one or two might have grown an inch!

Swordfish with Peas, page 200

A SUMMER DINNER

Fried Zucchini Blossoms*
Veal with Tuna Sauce*
Salad of Tender Summer Lettuce
Oranges with Mint*

The salad should be served separately as a course by itself, since the dressing would conflict with the tuna sauce. If possible, serve it without cheese, since the combination of salad greens with cheese is a poor invention and something I have been trying to fight for years. (No cheese is really enjoyable without wine, whereas all salad dressings destroy the taste of wine, no matter how little vinegar you use.)

I find that many people don't drink coffee in the evening, or they prefer decaffeinated. Now that there are some excellent decaffeinated coffees in the bean, make some ahead of time and offer it to your guests—hot or iced.

This is a meal that suits itself ideally for a good fruity white wine: a Montrachet, if you feel like splurging, or a Pinot Grigio. Or, if you like a really spicy wine, a Gewürztraminer.

Note: Zucchini blossoms are not easy to come by unless you live, or week-end, in the country. If you can't get them, serve a Zucchini and Spinach Flan (page 162) instead.

A FALL LUNCHEON

Tomato and Feta Cheese Salad*
Stuffed Crêpes*
Sugared Figs*

This is the kind of meal that gets a lot of compliments. It is unlikely that any of your guests has had any one of these dishes before, maybe with the exception of the Tomato and Feta Cheese Salad.

The reason why I consider it an ideal fall meal is that the large, juicy tomatoes we call "Beefsteak" should be in season. It makes a lot of difference, both in looks and in taste, whether you use puny, taste-less little tomatoes that have shivered through weeks of cold storage—which is what we get in the markets in winter and spring—or those lusty, bright red ones that we get in late summer or early fall.

Figs, of course, are only available in the fall, and even then they are a matter of luck. I suggest that you use this delicious dessert only for small luncheons; if you can find enough soft, ripe figs to serve 6 you are lucky, but it's worth a try. Of course, you ask your guests if they want regular or decaffeinated coffee.

Usually you would want to serve a red wine with the feta cheese, but with the crêpes I much prefer a white. The solution is to start serving wine only with the crêpes and choose a lively white—either a good Soave or a Pinot Chardonnay. There are some excellent ones from California.

A FALL DINNER

*Mushroom, Celery, Parmesan, and Truffle Salad**
*Poached Striped Bass or Red Snapper**
Boiled Potatoes
Buttered Green Beans
*Homemade Mayonnaise**
*Strawberry-Raspberry Mold**

This is a dinner of the utmost elegance. It might wreck you finan-cially, but it is worth it.

The main course and dessert can be prepared ahead of time, saving you a little time. At the conclusion, serve espresso in your most beautiful cups.

With a dinner of such magnitude, I would splurge on a Champagne. It need not be one of the greatest, provided it is brut. There are some lesser-known ones around that will send you to the poorhouse only for a little while.

A WINTER LUNCHEON

*Minestrone**
Assorted Cheeses
Fresh Fruit

Although this at first might appear too skimpy, eat it and then see if you feel like having much more after it.

With this meal, I'd serve some really good bread. I can't conceive of a lusty Minestrone served with an insipid pre-sliced, pre-packaged bread. Maybe you bake your own bread. Marvelous! If not you can probably buy some crusty whole wheat to chew with great gusto.

For the cheese, you'll find goat cheese is an acquired taste. I happen to love it and there are many different ones around these days. Add one to your repertoire of cheeses and serve pears with it. It is a delicious combination.

At the end, serve good strong, hot coffee and lots of it.

As for the wine, you really have a choice. A good Chianti, a Barolo from the region of Piedmont in Northern Italy, or—if it's a really cold, snowy day—a Barbera from the same region. It is the kind of wine you can almost chew.

A WINTER DINNER

*Mary's Meat Pie**
Mixed Salad of Belgian Endive, Mushrooms, and Avocado
*Dried Apricots and Peaches with Whipped Cream**

The meat pie is really a whole meal, and all it can stand is a salad. Serve the salad separately, or the dressing will run into the liquid from the pie and ruin both. The dressing for the salad should be a mild vinaigrette.

The dessert, though rich because of the cream, doesn't feel heavy. This is a case where the season dictates your menu. Who would plan a dessert of dried fruit, except in the winter?

In the evening, some people don't want coffee, but just ask: decaffeinated? Or perhaps your guests would like tea?

The meat pie needs a sturdy red wine. If you are in an Italian mood, a good Barolo of a certain age would be great. If you are in a French mood, you might opt for a Burgundy of medium age. And there are some excellent Cabernet Sauvignons from California.

RECIPES

HORS D'OEUVRE

Appetizers can be a nuisance. There you are, trying to cope with a main course and a complicated dessert, and you have to spend a lot of time preparing appetizers that go more or less unnoticed by your guests. You ask yourself: Can I get away with just potato chips and nuts? The answer is, you really can't. But your appetizers can be an addition to the meal that is homemade and special.

An unusual dip may be served surrounded with corn chips, however, thus avoiding the time-consuming washing and cutting up of vegetables for crudités. Fill a bowl with chips; your guests will munch on them in passing, as they would nuts. But you also need some simple hors d'oeuvre, and that is precisely what the following recipes are.

A Dip with Zip

1 pound skim milk ricotta   *5 ounces feta cheese*

Empty the ricotta onto a paper towel, cover with another paper towel, and let stand for 30 minutes or so to allow the moisture to be absorbed by the paper.

Place half the ricotta into a food processor; crumble half of the feta and add to the ricotta in the processor. Using the sharp blade, run the processor, turning it on and off until the cheeses are smooth and completely amalgamated. Scrape the mixture into a serving bowl and repeat with the remaining ricotta and feta. Add to the first batch, mix well, and refrigerate until well chilled.

Serves 10 to 16

NOTE: The reason for mixing the cheeses in two installments is that lumps are inevitable if the processor is too full at one time.

There are two different types of feta on the market: one sold pre-packaged, which is relatively mild; and one sold loose, which is very sharp indeed. The above quantity is for the mild type, so if you use the other, adjust the quantity according to your palate.

This mixture will keep in the refrigerator for 3 or more days. As it is a rather thick dip, serve it with corn chips or an equally hard cracker. If you wish to serve it with raw vegetables, cauliflower rosettes or hefty slices of fennel would be fine. Thin carrot sticks or little slivers of celery won't pick up the dip.

This dip has two advantages over the usual dips: it is lower in calories than the creamy ones, and most people are unable to guess what is in it.

Anchovy and Ricotta Spread

½ pound skim milk ricotta,
 preferably packaged type
1 tube (9 ounces) anchovy paste

2 tablespoons small capers (if
 mixture is used as a spread)

Place the ricotta on a paper towel and cover with another paper towel. Let stand for about 30 minutes. The paper will absorb the excess liquid.

Squeeze the anchovy paste into a bowl and add the ricotta a little at a time, mixing constantly. The anchovy and ricotta should be completely amalgamated.

If you use the mixture as a spread, make small heaps of it on little squares of dark bread and place a caper in the center of each. Refrigerate until you are ready to serve.

If you use the mixture as a dip, refrigerate until serving time, then place it on a tray surrounded with raw vegetables, such as cauliflower rosettes or snow peas.

Serves 6 to 8

NOTE: Using ricotta instead of the usual cream cheese in this and the following Roquefort spread makes for a much leaner mixture in keeping with the new tendency toward less rich foods. In addition, ricotta has a very different flavor, which makes the spread more interesting.

Roquefort Dip

½ pound skim milk ricotta
¼ pound Roquefort cheese, at
   room temperature

salt (optional)
about 2 tablespoons
   Worcestershire sauce

Place the ricotta on a paper towel and cover with another paper towel. Let stand for about 30 minutes. The paper will absorb the excess liquid.

Place the Roquefort in a bowl and crumble it with a fork. Add the ricotta a little at a time, beating constantly with the fork to amalgamate the 2 cheeses. When this is done and the mixture is a pretty, pale green, taste it. If you feel that a little salt is needed, add it. Add the Worcestershire sauce a little at a time until the mixture is seasoned to your taste. Add more ricotta if the mixture is too sharp.

If you plan to use this as a dip, serve it at room temperature surrounded by slices of peeled cucumber or unpeeled zucchini. If you plan to use it as a spread, refrigerate it and heap it on small squares of dark bread at the last moment.

There is one more, and most unusual, use for this mixture: sandwich a small spoonful between 2 walnut halves and serve as an hors d'oeuvre. These will have to be chilled before serving or the sandwiches will fall apart.

Serves 6 to 8

Miniature Sandwiches

1 cup pitted black olives
dark bread, sliced very thin

¼ pound soft chèvre (goat
  cheese)

The olives should be Greek, Italian, or Moroccan, meaning that they should be the shriveled kind (oil-cured) and very tasty, not smooth and glossy as are California olives. Chop them rather fine. If using a food processor, be careful not to purée them.

Cut the bread into 2½-inch squares, spread generously with the cheese, and sprinkle with the olives.

This is a delicious appetizer that looks like caviar. In fact, I call it the poor man's caviar. Or rather, that's what I used to call it . . . the price of goat cheese being what it is.

Serves about 20

NOTE: There are many goat cheeses on the market and I love them all. But for this appetizer you want a soft variety that spreads easily, like a Montrachet.

These sandwiches may be prepared way ahead of time and, unless it's a very hot day, don't need to be refrigerated. Just cover the squares with wax paper.

Eggplant and Mozzarella Sandwiches

3 small eggplants (called
    Italian eggplants in most
    markets)
1 large egg
flour
bread crumbs

¼ pound smoked mozzarella
    cheese
18 sweet basil leaves
oil for deep-frying
coarse salt to taste

Remove the tip and stem ends of the eggplants but don't peel the eggplants. Slice them lengthwise as thin as possible, discarding the outermost slices with a lot of peel. Each eggplant should yield about 6 slices; they don't have to be even in size, but try to match them up by size.

Beat the egg in a deep dish. Spread some flour (about 2 tablespoons) on a paper towel and then spread an equal amount of bread crumbs on another towel. Slice the mozzarella about 1/8 inch thick and cut each slice as necessary to cover about half an eggplant slice, placed in the center.

Start heating the oil in a large skillet, starting with a small amount of oil. Place a slice of eggplant in the flour, shake off the excess flour, then place it flat into the beaten egg. Put a basil leaf on top of the slice in the egg, cover the leaf with a slice of mozzarella, and then top with another basil leaf. Dip another eggplant slice in flour and place it on top of the basil leaf. Turn the sandwich over so both sides are well coated with beaten egg. Using a slotted spatula, gently place the sandwich in the bread crumbs, and turn it over to coat both sides; then place it in the hot oil and fry it. Allow one side to get very brown before turning the sandwich over; the eggplant has to be cooked through, and the sandwiches should be crisp and crackle when you bite into them. When the sandwich is browned (not burned), place it on a paper towel to absorb excess oil. Sprinkle with a little coarse salt, then continue with the other eggplant slices.

Serves 6 to 8

NOTE: If you live in a neighborhood where you can buy fresh smoked mozzarella, you are lucky; it will be soft and juicy. There is, however, a packaged smoked mozzarella that is quite acceptable. If that too is not available, use the plain mozzarella, but the sandwiches will be far less tasty.

■

Sardine Purée on Toast

1 medium mealy potato
1 can (3¾ ounces) sardines
1 hard-cooked egg yolk
2 tablespoons lemon juice

olive oil, if needed
4 slices bread
4 anchovy filets

Boil the potato in its skin. Unless your sardines are the skinless and boneless kind, skin them and remove the bones. Mash the sardines with a fork. Peel the boiled potato and mash it with the sardines. Add the egg yolk (keep the white to sprinkle, chopped, over spinach the next time you cook it). Add the lemon juice and mix well. If the mixture seems too stiff to spread you may beat in a few drops of olive oil. This happened to me only once when I had used a potato too large for the purpose.

Barely toast the bread and butter lightly enough to make the mixture stick to the bread; it shouldn't be too crisp. If you plan to serve the purée as an appetizer with drinks, cut each slice into 2 triangles. Spread the sardine mixture on them, cut the anchovy filets in half, and place a piece on top of the sardine mixture.

If you want to serve the toast as a first course for an informal dinner, leave the toasted bread whole, spread with purée, and top each with 1 anchovy filet. Place them very briefly under the broiler and serve immediately.

Serves 4

Pita and Mozzarella Canapés

6 small pita breads   *1 8-ounce piece mozzarella
cheese*

Flatten the pita breads with your hand and cut into small pie-shaped wedges.

Cut the mozzarella into hazelnut-sized chunks and place a chunk inside each wedge. Squeeze with your fingers to close. If the ends won't stay closed, don't worry; they will once they are hot. Place the wedges on a baking sheet, not too close together because the cheese tends to ooze.

A few minutes before serving, heat the oven to 400° and place the baking sheet in it for 2 to 3 minutes, or until the cheese has melted. Serve immediately.

Serves 20

NOTE: You need the small, toaster-sized pita breads for this recipe. If only large pita is available, cut triangles from the outer edges and save the center for other uses. However, this requires a little sense of geometry.

Cheese and Spinach Rolls

*20 large, flat leaves fresh
spinach*

*¼ pound creamy cheese, such as
Boursin or stracchino, at
room temperature*

Wash the spinach and dry thoroughly. Place about ½ teaspoon of cheese on one end of each leaf. Roll it up, secure with a toothpick, and serve with drinks.

Serves 5 to 6

NOTE: This is the invention of a friend of mine, which I have copied shamelessly. It is so simple that I don't understand why I hadn't thought of it. The only difficulty is in finding the right cheese. It should be creamy, slightly sticky, and of course tasty. Cream cheese won't do at all. You might try Roquefort, made creamy with a little butter.

And be sure you use tender young spinach. Those large curly leaves are brittle and won't roll up.

Cheese Rolls

12 Parker House rolls
½ pound mixed cheeses (⅛
   pound each of Gouda, Edam,
   swiss, and fontina)

1 cup thick white sauce made
   with a pinch of nutmeg

Tear off a small piece from the narrow end of each roll. With your fingers, remove as much of the center as possible, leaving the outside intact. (Save the centers to make bread crumbs or use them in a bread pudding.)

Cube the cheeses, place in the top of a double boiler over very low heat, and allow them to melt slowly.

Preheat the oven to 350°.

Add the melted cheese to the white sauce and amalgamate well. Working quickly, fill the rolls with the mixture before it hardens. Place the rolls on a baking sheet and heat in the oven for about 10 minutes. Serve warm.

Serves 6

NOTE: The rolls may be prepared ahead of time and heated just before serving. They may be served as a rather substantial appetizer with drinks, or as a first course, or instead of cheese at the end of a meal.

Mushroom Caps with Tuna Mayonnaise

20 large fresh mushrooms
1 cup mayonnaise, preferably
    homemade (page 194)
1 can (7 ounces) tuna, well
    drained

½ teaspoon dry English
    mustard
1 tablespoon capers

Remove the mushroom stems and reserve for other use. If the caps are very white and clean, wipe them with a damp cloth. If they have small blemishes, peel them with a sharp knife or with your hands by pulling off the top skin starting under the caps. (Don't buy mushrooms with a lot of blemishes.)

Mix the mayonnaise, tuna and mustard in a blender or food processor. The mixture must be very well amalgamated.

Fill the mushroom caps with the tuna mayonnaise, place a caper in the center of each cap, and chill well before serving.

Serves 6 to 8

Eggs alla Cipriani

6 eggs
1 cup homemade mayonnaise
(made without mustard or
lemon juice, page 194)

pinch of salt
1 teaspoon ground cinnamon

Bring water to a strong boil in a saucepan. Carefully lower the eggs into the water, using a spoon. Allow to boil for exactly 12 minutes. Remove from heat and place under cold running water.

As soon as eggs are cool enough to handle, peel and halve them. Remove the yolks and place them in a bowl. Add 1 tablespoon of mayonnaise and mash the yolks, mixing them with the mayonnaise. Add the salt and mix well.

Fill the whites with the mixture and place them, cut side down, on individual plates. Allow 3 halves per person. Cover with the remaining mayonnaise, which should be rather thin. Sprinkle with cinnamon, being careful that each egg gets more or less the same amount.

Serves 4

NOTE: I was served these eggs at La Locanda Cipriani at Asolo, in Northern Italy. Even for them, it was a novelty. We have all served eggs sprinkled with pepper or curry powder. Cinnamon is an entirely different taste experience.

These eggs may be served as part of an hors d'oeuvre or by themselves, on a bed of finely shredded endive, as a simple first course.

FIRST COURSES AND LIGHT MAIN DISHES

F irst courses are a specialty of mine. They are so versatile, and many times you can simply double the recipe and serve them as a main dish for lunch.

Most first courses are easy to make and don't require much time. Take the fish mousse: It's easy to make, looks elegant, and is easily doubled to serve as a main course for a summer luncheon (make two molds instead of one).

Very few first courses require many hours over a hot stove, and very few also require that you light the oven and keep it going for hours on a hot day. Not all are inexpensive, but they all immediately set the mood for an elegant dinner.

Chilled Tomato Soup

2 large ripe tomatoes or 3 cups
*   peeled canned tomatoes*
2 cups chicken or beef broth
1 cup tomato juice
1 teaspoon grated lemon rind
*   (zest only)*

⅓ cup dry sherry
1 teaspoon Worcestershire sauce
1 tablespoon finely chopped
*   chives*

Peel and seed the tomatoes and chop coarse, being careful to retain their liquid. The best way to do this is to chop them in a shallow bowl.

Bring the broth to a boil and add the tomato juice and chopped tomatoes. Return the soup to a boil, cover, and simmer over very low heat for about 30 minutes. Remove from heat, stir in the lemon rind, and let cool completely.

Add the sherry and refrigerate.

Just before serving stir in the Worcestershire sauce. The soup may be served in individual cups or bowls or in a tureen. Either way, sprinkle with chives at the last minute.

Serves 6

Chilled Leek and Potato Soup

2 large leeks
2 large mealy potatoes
3 tablespoons unsalted butter
4 cups chicken broth

1 small bunch chives (bunch
  about 1 inch thick)
salt and freshly ground white
  pepper to taste

Trim the leeks and discard the green part. Cut the leeks in half lengthwise and rinse thoroughly under cold running water to remove all traces of sand. Cut them into pieces and purée in a food processor. Pour or scrape leek purée into a large bowl.

Peel the potatoes, cut into chunks, purée them in the food processor, and add to the leeks.

Melt the butter in a deep saucepan and add the leeks and potatoes. Cook briefly, stirring constantly, and add the broth. Cover and let simmer for about 30 minutes.

Chop ½ bunch of chives very fine and add to the broth. Taste and season with salt and pepper.

Refrigerate the soup and, just before serving, chop the remaining chives fine and sprinkle on top.

Serves 6 to 8

NOTE: If you want a richer soup, you may add 1 cup of light cream and mix well before refrigerating.

Barley-Ham Soup

2 tablespoons lard
½ cup chopped cured ham
½ cup barley

4 cups beef broth (chicken broth
 may be used, but the soup
 will be less flavorful)
2 egg yolks (optional)

Melt the lard over medium heat and stir in the chopped ham. Add the barley and sauté for a couple of minutes, stirring to coat well. Add the broth and bring to a simmer. Cover the saucepan and simmer gently until the barley is tender. Test the soup after about 30 minutes. The barley should not be allowed to get mushy but should be *al dente*.

Remove the soup from the heat.

Beat the egg yolks and swirl them into the soup.

This soup may be prepared hours before serving and may be gently reheated, but should not be allowed to boil.

Serves 6 to 8

NOTE: If barley doesn't appeal to you, buckwheat may be used instead. (Buckwheat is also called kasha, and is readily available in most markets.)

The preparation of the soup is the same as for barley, but cooking time should be reduced to about 6 minutes, or until the buckwheat is tender.

Bread Soup

1 loaf French or Italian bread
   (not seeded)
1 quart broth, canned or
   homemade
½ cup olive oil

pinch of oregano
salt and pepper if desired
½ cup freshly grated Parmesan
   cheese

Cut the bread into chunks, place the chunks in a bowl, and add the broth. Let stand for at least 1 hour. If the bread has absorbed all the broth, add another cup.

Mash the bread mush with a wooden spoon and transfer to a saucepan. Place on medium heat and simmer, mixing frequently to keep the bread from sticking to the bottom of the pot. After about 15 minutes, add the oil, stir, and simmer a few minutes longer. Add the oregano and taste to see if salt is needed. You will probably want to add a little pepper.

If you plan to serve the soup immediately, transfer it to a tureen or to individual bowls and sprinkle the Parmesan on top. If you plan to serve it later, don't add the cheese at this point. The soup may be served hot or cold.

Serves 6 to 8

NOTE: This is also an excellent way to use up leftover bread from your party.

Zesty Onion Soup

5 medium white onions
2 tablespoons unsalted butter
1 tablespoon all-purpose flour
1 cup milk
2 quarts broth, preferably beef

freshly ground pepper to taste
½ cup freshly grated Parmesan
 cheese
10 slices white bread (optional)

Peel the onions. Cut 4 of them in half and then slice them as thin as possible.

Melt the butter in a large pot, add the onions, and stir. Cook until the onions are wilted and transparent, but not brown. Reduce the heat to very low and add the flour, sifted through a small sieve stirring to prevent lumps. Add the milk and stir, then gradually add the broth. Cover and simmer.

Cut the remaining onion into chunks, place them in a food processor, and purée. If you don't have a food processor, chop the onion as fine as you can. Add the onion to the broth, taste, and add the pepper.

The longer this soup simmers, the better. In fact, it is at its best 24 hours after it has stopped simmering. When you are about ready to serve, add the Parmesan.

If you wish, toast the bread slices and place 1 slice in each soup plate. Ladle the soup over it.

I usually serve the soup as is, accompanied by crusty bread.

Serves 10

NOTE: Adding the puréed onion is my variation. It gives the soup a slightly creamy quality.

On a cold winter night this is a splendid dish. For the following 12 hours be sure not to talk to anyone who hasn't eaten it. Onions, you know.

Fish Mousse

1 envelope unflavored gelatin
¼ cup cold water
¼ cup hot consommé
1 cup flaked canned tuna,
    salmon, or crabmeat
½ cup finely chopped celery
    heart, including a few leaves
1 cup mayonnaise, preferably
    homemade (page 194)

2 tablespoons chopped capers
    plus 1 teaspoon whole capers
1 tablespoon Worcestershire
    sauce
lemon wedges (optional)
2 hard-cooked eggs, sliced
    (optional)

Sprinkle the gelatin on the cold water and allow to soften for about 10 minutes. Add the hot consommé and stir to dissolve the gelatin.

In a food processor blend the fish, celery, mayonnaise, and chopped capers, and spoon the mixture into a mixing bowl. Add the gelatin and Worcestershire, and mix well.

Rinse a fish-shaped mold with cold water, pour the mousse in, and level the surface with the back of a spoon.

Chill for at least 2 hours. Unmold just before serving and scatter the whole capers on top. You may surround the mousse with lemon wedges and slices of hard-cooked eggs.

Serves 6

Tuna or Salmon Layered Mousse

2 cups chicken broth	¾ cup mayonnaise, preferably
1½ envelopes unflavored gelatin	homemade (page 194)
1 can (7 ounces) tuna or	1 tablespoon brandy
salmon	lemon slices and sprigs of
4 anchovy filets	parsley for decoration

Heat the broth and sprinkle the gelatin over it. Mix until totally dissolved, then let stand to cool.

Break up the tuna or salmon with a fork and place in the bowl of a food processor. Add the anchovies and process until puréed. Remove from the food processor and transfer to a bowl. Add the mayonnaise and the brandy. Mix well.

Pour half the broth in a 7½-inch soufflé dish and chill until slightly jelled. Spread the tuna-mayonnaise mixture over it. Gently pour the other half of the broth over the mixture and refrigerate for at least 1 hour, more if needed. Unmold onto a serving platter and decorate with slices of lemon and sprigs of parsley.

Serves 4

NOTE: I say "7½-inch soufflé dish" because that is precisely the standard size. If you want to call it 8 inches, that's fine too.

Tomatoes and Mozzarella

8 very large ripe tomatoes
coarse salt
1 pound fresh mozzarella cheese
(see note)

freshly ground black pepper
½ cup olive oil
1 large bunch fresh basil

Dip the tomatoes into boiling water, peel, and cut them into even slices. Place them on a platter, sprinkle with salt, and let them stand for an hour or so. They will shed their water and most of their seeds. Arrange the slices on a large platter, overlapping slightly.

Slice the mozzarella in half lengthwise, then cut the 2 halves crosswise into slices a little smaller than the slices of tomatoes. Place 1 slice of mozzarella between every 2 slices of tomatoes. Grind fresh pepper over them. Pour the oil over them and let stand for about 30 minutes. If they stand a little longer it will do no harm. Just keep them away from heat. At the moment of serving, chop the basil coarse and scatter it over the surface.

Serves 10 to 12

NOTE: When I say "fresh mozzarella" I mean the kind that is kept in water, not the packaged type. If it is not available, forget this recipe. Packaged mozzarella, though good for many uses, does nothing for this dish. But if you can get the fresh kind, this dish won't be missing on any of your summer buffets. It takes no time to prepare, it is delicious, and it looks lovely.

Tomatoes Stuffed with Corn and Pineapple

6 ripe tomatoes, unblemished
   and as close to uniform size
   as possible
1 cup cooked corn kernels
1 cup fresh pineapple cubes

freshly ground black pepper to
   taste
½ cup mayonnaise, preferably
   homemade (page 194)
6 Boston lettuce leaves
   (optional)

Cut a slice off the top of the tomatoes. Place them, cut side down, on a platter and let stand for at least 30 minutes.

Mix the corn with the pineapple, making sure both are well drained. Add the pepper and mayonnaise, and mix.

Turn the tomatoes cut side up; they should have shed their liquid and most of their seeds. Remove any remaining seeds with a small spoon and, at the same time, press down on the flesh to make as much room for the stuffing as possible. With the small spoon fill them with the corn-pineapple mixture, pressing down so that you get as much stuffing in as possible. There should be a little mound on top. Chill and serve on a platter or individual plates. If the tomatoes are not very large or don't stand up properly by themselves, place a leaf of Boston lettuce under each.

Serves 6

NOTE: Although the combination of corn and pineapple did not appeal to me at first, I have come to like it. This dish originated in a very good New York restaurant where it is very popular.

Tomatoes Stuffed with Blue Cheese

3 large ripe tomatoes
salt
¼ pound Roquefort or other
   blue cheese

2 tablespoons butter
1 teaspoon Worcestershire sauce
about 1 tablespoon brandy
Boston lettuce leaves

Cut the tomatoes in half crosswise, sprinkle with salt, and turn upside down on a plate. Let stand for about 10 minutes to drain.

Both the cheese and the butter should be at room temperature. Mix them well and add the Worcestershire sauce and the brandy, a few drops at a time. The mixture should be thick and creamy.

Turn the tomatoes cut side up. Remove any seeds that remain and stuff the tomatoes with the cheese mixture, pressing down with a small spoon to fill the cavity completely.

Refrigerate if you wish, but remove them from the refrigerator 30 minutes before serving.

Place them on a platter, surrounded by lettuce leaves, or serve on individual plates.

This is a rather filling appetizer. One half tomato per person is enough.

Serves 6

Asparagus and Prosciutto Bundles

2 pounds fresh asparagus
4 tablespoons unsalted butter
12 very thin slices prosciutto

½ cup freshly grated
Parmesan cheese
2 tablespoons bread crumbs
(preferably homemade)

Wash the asparagus, cut off and discard the tough ends of the stalks. Cook the asparagus in rapidly simmering water until barely tender. (Cooking time can't be given as it depends upon the size of the asparagus.) Drain the asparagus before the stalks are limp. The cooking liquid may be reserved for stock.

While the asparagus is cooking, use some of the butter to grease a rectangular ovenproof serving dish. Melt the remaining butter. Preheat the oven to 350°.

Spread the prosciutto on a board. Spread half the Parmesan on a paper towel. Dip the well-drained asparagus, 1 at a time, in the melted butter and then in the Parmesan. The more cheese clings to them the better. Place 3 or 4 (according to thickness) asparagus on one end of a slice of prosciutto and roll them up. You will have 12 prosciutto "bundles."

Place bundles side by side in the serving dish. Mix the remaining Parmesan with the bread crumbs and sprinkle over the bundles. Pour the remaining butter over them and bake for 10 to 12 minutes, or until the bread crumbs are golden. Serve hot.

Serves 6

NOTE: If prosciutto is just too elusive, you may substitute boiled ham, but don't expect quite the same result. Also, don't try this recipe with anything less than the freshest of the season's asparagus; when asparagus are not at their best, stay away from this recipe.

Anchovies and Potatoes

4 large potatoes, preferably
   Idaho
2 large firm tomatoes, preferably
   beefsteak
10 anchovy filets

¼ cup minced fresh basil
⅓ cup olive oil
juice of 1 lemon
freshly ground pepper to taste
basil leaves for garnish

Clean the potatoes, boil them in their jackets until tender, and let cool slightly. Dip the tomatoes briefly into boiling water, then peel, slice, and let stand for about 30 minutes. They will shed some of their liquid, and you can help them shed some of their seeds. Beefsteak tomatoes are recommended because they have few seeds.

When the potatoes are cool enough to handle, peel and cut them into slices about 1/3 inch thick. Layer half the potatoes in the bottom of a large shallow bowl. Place half the anchovies at regular intervals on top of the potatoes. Cover with the remaining potatoes and arrange the remaining anchovies on top. Sprinkle the minced basil over the anchovies and arrange the tomato slices in an overlapping circular design on top.

Mix the oil with the lemon juice until well amalgamated and pour the mixture over the tomatoes. This should be done well ahead of time to give the flavors a chance to mingle. Just before serving, grind a little pepper over the top and garnish with the basil leaves.

Serves 6

NOTE: I include this dish as an appetizer. It can also be a savory first course for an informal dinner, or a colorful addition to a buffet table. A glass bowl will show it to its best advantage. For a party touch, slice 5 or 6 large raw mushroom caps and scatter them over the top.

Broiled Oak Mushrooms

6 large fresh (shiitake) oak
   mushrooms
½ cup olive oil

coarse salt to taste
parsley

Remove the stems from the mushrooms and reserve for another use (in a stew or a risotto). Wipe the caps carefully with a damp towel. If any sand clings to them, rinse briefly under cold water and immediately pat dry.

Heat the broiler. Oil a baking sheet and place the mushroom caps on it, top side down. Trickle some olive oil over each cap and place under the broiler, not more than 5 inches from the heat. Watch them carefully; they must not burn. After about 1 minute, remove mushrooms from the broiler and turn over. If the baking sheet has dried, add some oil and trickle some over the top sides of the mushrooms. Place them again under the broiler and broil for another minute or so. (The cooking time depends upon the thickness of the caps.) Pierce caps with a fork; if they pierce easily, they are done.

Remove mushrooms from broiler and add another trickle of oil. Sprinkle with coarse salt and serve hot with just a sprig of parsley as decoration.

Serves 6

NOTE: These marvelous brown mushrooms, so similar to the mushrooms of my native Italy, have recently appeared in many markets. The caps are 6 to 7 inches in diameter and one cap per person is plenty when served as an appetizer.

If you are lucky and have grapevine in your garden or live close to a vineyard, pick 6 large, glossy grape leaves and wash them carefully (they have probably been sprayed). Dry the leaves and place them under the mushroom caps before you broil them. Serve the mushrooms atop their leaves. This might sound like an affectation, but the leaves add a very special aroma. In Italy we would call this dish *Funghi alla Vigna.*

Chicken with Mushrooms and Tomatoes, page 204

Eggplant Birds

2 medium eggplants
salt
6 tablespoons corn or sunflower
    oil
¼ pound boiled ham

1 large egg
3 tablespoons freshly grated
    Parmesan cheese
about 2 tablespoons bread
    crumbs
freshly ground pepper to taste

Cut the unpeeled eggplants into thin slices lengthwise. Sprinkle them with salt and let stand on a paper towel to drain.

Heat 4 tablespoons of the oil in a skillet and fry the eggplant slices a few at a time in order not to crowd them. Don't allow them to brown. As soon as they have lost their raw look, place them on a paper towel to absorb excess oil.

Chop the ham as fine as possible. This is most easily done in a food processor as the ham should be almost puréed. Beat the egg in a bowl, add the ham and the cheese, and mix well. Add enough bread crumbs to give a fairly thick consistency. Taste the mixture and add salt and pepper, if you wish. Mix well.

Place about 1 teaspoon of the mixture in the center of each eggplant slice. Roll up the slices and secure with toothpicks.

Heat the remaining oil in the skillet and fry the "birds" over high heat, turning to brown on all sides. With a spatula, transfer to a heated serving platter.

Serves 4 to 6

NOTE: This dish may be prepared ahead of time until the last step, the frying of the "birds." The completed dish can be placed on an oven proof platter and kept in a lukewarm oven for a little while.

Eggplant birds are also a good main course for a light lunch with steamed rice on the side.

Eggplant Stew

6 small eggplants, preferably
  pear-shaped
salt
½ cup olive oil
1 clove garlic, chopped fine
  (optional)
4 large ripe tomatoes, peeled
  and seeded, or 4½ cups
  canned tomatoes

2 tablespoons coarsely chopped
  fresh basil
3 tablespoons freshly grated
  Parmesan cheese
freshly ground pepper
4 large eggs

Cut the unpeeled eggplants crosswise into fairly thin slices. Sprinkle lightly with salt and let stand on a paper towel for about 20 minutes. They will shed some of their water, and the salt will disappear with it.

Heat the oil in a large skillet, preferably cast-iron, over high heat. Add the garlic, if desired. When the oil is very hot, add the eggplant slices. Turn them with a spatula so they cook on both sides. As soon as they look translucent, lower the heat to medium and add the tomatoes, mashing them slightly with a wooden spoon. Add the chopped basil. Let simmer for about 10 minutes. If the mixture gets a little dry, cover the skillet.

After about 20 minutes total cooking time, add the cheese and mix. Taste and add salt and pepper, if desired. Beat the eggs in a bowl, add them to the skillet, and stir quickly. Remove from the heat and serve immediately.

Serves 6

NOTE: This dish may be prepared in advance except for the addition of the eggs. It is one of those recipes that result from the horrendous price of meat in Europe. If you want to make it even more economical, use grated domestic swiss cheese instead of Parmesan. The result is not quite the same, but it's a lot cheaper.

Stuffed Peppers

3⅓ cups water
salt
1 cup long-grain rice
1 large ripe tomato or 2 peeled
*   canned tomatoes*

6 anchovy filets
½ cup oil
6 green bell peppers, preferably
*   all the same size*
3 tablespoons unsalted butter

Preheat the oven to 375°.

Bring 3 cups of water to a boil in a large saucepan and salt it lightly. Add the rice and cook for about 15 minutes, stirring frequently. Drain the rice and let it cool.

Peel, seed, and drain the fresh tomato. Chop it (or the canned tomatoes, if you are using them) coarsely. Add the tomato pulp to the rice.

Chop the anchovies and add them to the rice, along with 3 table-spoons of the oil.

Core the peppers and remove the seeds, being careful not to break the peppers. Fill each with the rice mixture.

Butter an ovenproof casserole large enough to hold the peppers upright but not so large that they will topple over. Mix 3 table-spoons of the oil with the remaining ⅓ cup water and pour the mix-ture gently around the peppers. Pour the remaining oil over the peppers and dot them with the butter. Place peppers in the oven and bake for about 25 minutes. Check after 20 minutes; if they are very young, they might already be done.

Serves 6

NOTE: If you want to serve these peppers as a main course for an informal luncheon, allow 2 per person. They are good hot, but even better cold, so try them that way too.

Caution: don't oversalt the water for the rice; the anchovies add enough salt to this dish.

Basic Crêpes

1 cup milk
½ cup water
¾ cup all-purpose flour
salt to taste
3 large eggs

pinch of freshly grated nutmeg
   (optional)
1 tablespoon unsalted butter, at
   room temperature

Mix the milk and water in a large bowl, then sift in the flour and salt. Using a wire whisk, beat until the ingredients are well amalgamated. Add the eggs 1 at a time, beating until each is well absorbed. Add the nutmeg, if desired. Let the mixture stand for at least 30 minutes. If a few lumps are visible when you are ready to make the crêpes, whisk the mixture again until smooth.

Take an 8-inch omelet pan and make sure the inside is perfectly clean and shiny. (If you feel more at ease with a smaller pan, go ahead and use it. The important thing is to use a pan you are familiar with—we all have one pan that is like an old friend.)

With one corner of a paper towel, pick up a little of the softened butter and rub it all over the inside of the pan. Place the pan over fairly high heat. Pour about 1/3 of an average-size ladle of the batter into the pan and tilt it immediately. The batter should cover the bottom of the pan, but not the sides. As the batter begins to bubble, loosen the edge with a thin spatula and shake the pan to make sure the crêpe doesn't stick to the bottom. Have a large platter handy and, when the edges of the crêpe are golden, turn the pan upside down so that the crêpe falls on the platter.

Pick up another bit of butter with your towel and repeat the operation. By the time the second crêpe has landed on the platter, the first one will be cool enough to handle. Delicately place it back in the lightly greased pan, brown side up, and allow it to bake on the other side. Keep the pan lightly greased with the buttered paper towel and continue, baking the crêpes on both sides until all the batter is used up.

Yields 10 large or 12 small crêpes

NOTE: This is my way of making crêpes, but I am sure many of you have your own method. Use the system you like best and remember that crêpes freeze well. Just let them cool, then stack the crêpes, separating each with a piece of wax paper. Cover the whole bundle tightly with aluminum foil and place in the freezer. Don't forget them though; they won't last forever, but I have kept them frozen for a month or so and they were quite happy. Once out of the freezer they defrost in a few minutes.

■

Stuffed Crêpes

1 tablespoon unsalted butter
6 large eggs, lightly beaten
3 tablespoons heavy cream

salt and pepper to taste
pinch of freshly grated nutmeg
12 small crêpes, about 5 inches
in diameter

Preheat the oven to 350°.

Melt the butter in a skillet over medium heat. Add the eggs and lower the heat. As soon as the eggs begin to set, add the cream, salt, and pepper and stir quickly and lightly as you would for scrambled eggs. While the eggs are still soft and creamy, remove them from the heat and grate a little nutmeg over them.

Place the crêpes on a flat surface and place a spoonful of the eggs on the lower half of each crêpe. Roll the crêpes as you would a jelly roll, taking care not to let the eggs ooze out. Place the filled crêpes in a buttered baking dish, bake for about 5 minutes, and serve.

Serves 6

NOTE: This is an ideal luncheon dish or first course for dinner, particularly if you have little time, little help, and little money.

The crêpes may be made days ahead of time and frozen. They may be stuffed an hour or so before serving, but remember: if the are very cold, they will require more than 5 minutes in the oven. If you wish, you may dot them with butter and sprinkle with Parmesan before baking. (I don't.)

Broken Omelet

4 tablespoons all-purpose flour
1 cup milk
2 extra large eggs or 3 large
  eggs

½ teaspoon salt
3 tablespoons unsalted butter

Mix the flour, milk and eggs in a bowl, using a wire whisk. Let stand for at least 30 minutes. If there are any little lumps, mix some more. Stir in the salt.

Using an iron skillet if you have one, melt 2 tablespoons of the butter over medium heat. As soon as the butter is melted (don't allow it to brown), pour the batter in. It should start to set immediately. With a spatula, lift the edges constantly to allow the batter to run to the bottom of the skillet.

As soon as the mixture is solid, start cutting it into bite-sized pieces with the edge of the spatula. When the omelet is all cut up, lower the heat and cover for a few minutes. Lift the lid; the pieces will have grown in size. Cut them some more and turn them while doing so. Cover again for a few minutes. When you lift the lid, the pieces should have brown edges. Fry a couple of minutes longer, uncovered. Meanwhile, place the remaining tablespoon of butter on a heated platter, add the "broken omelet," toss, and serve very hot, accompanied by a salad.

Serves 4

NOTE: This is a delicious and very simple dish your guests might like to watch you prepare, particularly if you are in a country kitchen at lunchtime. The whole operation takes about 10 minutes. (One of your guests can heat the platter for you under hot running water while you finish frying the egg mixture.)

I have known this dish all my life, I think. I gave it the name "broken omelet" when I was about 6 years old; I watched a cook prepare it and thought she didn't know how to make an omelet! Only very recently have I discovered that it is a well-known dish of Swiss origin. And it has a real name: *tac*. The "c" is pronounced as in cherry.

I like "broken omelet" better.

Quiche without a Crust

1½ cups ricotta, whole milk or skim
1 cup lukewarm water
6 slices white bread, including crust, stale or fresh
⅓ cup plus 2 tablespoons freshly grated Parmesan cheese
about 1 teaspoon salt
about 1 teaspoon freshly ground pepper
1 large egg
1 tablespoon finely chopped fresh basil
1 teaspoon finely chopped parsley
2 teaspoons unsalted butter

Place the ricotta on a paper towel, cover with another paper towel, and let stand for about 30 minutes. The towels will absorb the moisture.

Pour the water into a bowl and add the bread. Let stand until the bread has absorbed the water and has turned to mush. Squeeze out the water with your hands.

Preheat the oven to 400°.

Place bread and ricotta in a large bowl and mix well. Add the ⅓ cup of Parmesan, salt, and pepper and mix well. Add the egg, mix well, and stir in the basil and parsley.

Use a little of the butter to grease an 8-inch pie dish that is about 1½ inches deep. Pour the mixture into the dish. With the back of a spoon, flatten the surface so it is even. Sprinkle with the remaining Parmesan and dot with the remaining butter. Bake for about 20 minutes, or until the top is golden.

Serves 6

NOTE: Ricotta is a bland fresh cheese sold in most supermarkets in plastic containers. It comes in 2 types: whole milk and part skim milk. Either is suitable for this dish, though the whole milk ricotta makes a richer quiche. It may be served hot or at room temperature, or even cold. I find it best at room temperature. It may be baked ahead of time and briefly placed in the oven before serving. It cannot be frozen.

Ricotta and Mushroom Mold

1 pound skim milk ricotta
3 tablespoons butter
1 cup cleaned and sliced fresh
  mushrooms
4 eggs, separated and at room
  temperature

salt (optional)
½ cup plus 2 tablespoons freshly
  grated Parmesan cheese
pinch of nutmeg
freshly ground pepper to taste

Preheat the oven to 400°.

Empty the ricotta onto a paper towel and cover with a second towel. Let stand for at least 30 minutes or until the paper has absorbed the excess moisture.

Melt 1 tablespoon butter in a skillet and add the mushrooms. Cook briefly, covered, over high heat.

Place the ricotta in a large bowl. Add the egg yolks and the mushrooms, salt, nutmeg, and ½ cup Parmesan cheese. Mix until amalgamated and smooth.

Butter an 8-inch soufflé dish.

Beat the egg whites until stiff peaks form, then fold into the ricotta mixture, using a spatula and incorporating the whites a little at a time. Sprinkle a little pepper over the top, then sprinkle the remaining Parmesan over. Dot with the remaining butter and place in the hot oven. Bake for about 20 minutes or until the top is golden and puffy. Serve at once.

Serves 6

NOTE: This won't puff up quite like a regular cheese soufflé because the ricotta mixture is heavier than a basic soufflé mixture, but it will be delicious for hours even after it has cooled.

Spinach and Zucchini Flan

1 pound tender fresh spinach
3 or 4 small zucchini (no longer
   than 5 or 6 inches), washed
   and tips trimmed
½ cup coarsely chopped pitted
   imported black olives

1½ teaspoons freshly ground
   black pepper
⅓ cup olive oil
8 eggs
1 cup freshly grated Parmesan
   cheese

Preheat the oven to 350°.

Wash the spinach repeatedly in lukewarm water. Lifting it out of the water instead of pouring it into a container, because you will pour the sand with it. With only the water that clings to the leaves, place the spinach in a saucepan and cook for 5 to 6 minutes, depending on the size of the leaves. In another saucepan, cook the zucchini about 4 minutes; they should be *al dente*.

When the spinach is done, pour it into a colander and run cold water over to prevent it from cooking further. As soon as it is cool enough to handle, squeeze every bit of water out with your hands; it's the only way to get it really dry. When the zucchini are cooked, let them cool and then slice them to the thickness of a silver dollar.

Spread the spinach on the bottom of a rectangular or oval baking dish, good looking enough to come to the table. Scatter the olives over the spinach and cover with the zucchini slices. Sprinkle the pepper over all, and pour the oil over the mixture in a thin stream.

In a large bowl, beat the eggs with half the Parmesan and pour the mixture evenly over the vegetables. Place in the oven and bake for about 20 to 25 minutes. The eggs should be set but not petrified. Remove from the oven and sprinkle the remaining Parmesan evenly over the surface while the dish is hot. The Parmesan will melt slightly and make a nice crust. Let cool and serve cold or at room temperature. (I also enjoy it hot.)

Serves 6

NOTE: This is not actually a flan, but I was at a loss as to what to call it. It's a childhood recipe that for us was simply "that thing with spinach." We hated it, and we tried to come home from school late, so the grown-ups would have eaten. Now we love that thing with spinach.

Basic Frittata

6 large eggs
2 tablespoons butter
2 tablespoons olive oil (more if
   needed)

salt and pepper to taste
freshly grated Parmesan cheese
   (optional)

Beat the eggs in a porcelain or pottery bowl just to the point at which whites and yolks are perfectly amalgamated, but not foamy. (Overbeating would cause the frittata to toughen.) Stir in the salt and pepper.

Melt half the butter in an iron skillet or in an omelet pan over medium-high heat. Add half the oil and allow it to get very hot but not brown. Add the eggs and as soon as the edges begin to set, lower the heat. With a small spatula, lift the edges to allow the uncooked egg to run toward the center of the frittata, and push the edges slightly to the center of the skillet. The frittata should be quite thick in the middle. Make sure it doesn't stick to the bottom of the pan.

Lift the edge to see if it is brown underneath. If it is, invert the frittata onto a plate, cooked side up. This requires a little skill: place the plate, which should be a little larger than the frittata but smaller than the skillet, over the skillet and, with one hand over the plate and the other hand grasping the handle of the skillet, turn the skillet upside down. The frittata should land on the plate in perfect condition. If it doesn't work perfectly the first time, don't give up; it will.

Add the rest of the butter and oil to the skillet and slide the frittata, uncooked side down, back into it. Brown for a few minutes, then slide it onto a serving platter. That's easy!

Sprinkle the top with a little Parmesan, if you wish.

Serves 4 to 6

NOTE: As I said, this is the basic frittata. It has almost infinite variations.

If it is in season, sprinkle finely chopped basil over the frittata before you turn it. Bits of cheese may be added, as well as small pieces of salami. The important thing to remember is: whatever you add should be sprinkled over the frittata while it is still quite soft.

A frittata can be served either hot or cold. When hot, it is soft and quite thick, an ideal luncheon dish served with a salad, or a first course for dinner. When cold, it gets quite flat but is still delicious for picnics or in sandwiches as school lunch for the kids.

La Spadellata

1 pound spaghetti, preferably
  imported
½ pint light cream
1 teaspoon tomato paste

salt and pepper (optional)
3 tablespoons freshly grated
  Parmesan cheese

This is an ideal dish for those who have a chafing dish and like to put a finishing touch on the food they serve their guests.

Cook the spaghetti in salted water until al dente.

While the spaghetti is cooking, heat a deep skillet or the pan of a chafing dish. Pour in the cream and as it heats, dissolve the tomato paste in the cream.

Drain the spaghetti and add to the cream-tomato mixture. Toss carefully but vigorously. Add the Parmesan and toss again. Serve immediately, while piping hot.

Serves 6

NOTE: There is an excellent pasta on the market imported from Italy, which comes from a small town called Fara S. Martino. It has the advantage over other pastas in that it takes exactly 10 minutes to cook the spaghetti (smaller pastas take less time), which gives you time to prepare the cream mixture and to get your guests to the table.

Should you have pasta leftover from a recent dinner party, there's a simply delicious way to use it up: Spaghetti Crêpes! Place a tablespoon of butter in a cast-iron skillet and let it melt. When the butter is hot, drop about 1 cup (tightly packed) cooked spaghetti into it. Stir and allow the spaghetti to get well coated with the butter. (Don't worry if your spaghetti was originally prepared with cheese or a sauce—use it in this recipe anyway.) Pour a ¼ cup of crêpe batter (see page 156) over the spaghetti; the batter will set almost immediately and will make a thick crêpe. Turn the crêpe with a spatula and allow it to get golden. Add about 2 tablespoons of freshly grated Parmesan cheese and serve hot or at room temperature. This crêpe is big enough to serve 2 or 3 persons; if you have more than 1 cup of leftover pasta, simply increase the amount of crêpe batter proportionately. I doubt that you will have even 1 strand of spaghetti left from a Spadellata, but if you do it makes a great-looking crêpe—pink and yellow.

Buckwheat Noodles with Olive Sauce

1 pound buckwheat noodles
1 tablespoon salt
½ cup pure olive oil

3 tablespoons olive purée (see note)
⅓ cup freshly grated Parmesan cheese (optional)

Bring about 6 quarts of water to a strong boil in a large pot and add the salt. Stir in the noodles and cook, stirring frequently, until they are done al dente.

Meanwhile, heat the oil in a skillet, add the olive purée and stir until the purée is totally dissolved in the oil. Don't bring to a boil. Pour the mixture into a warm porcelain or pottery serving bowl.

Drain the cooked noodles and quickly add to the heated bowl. Toss enthusiastically to coat the noodles well with the olive sauce. Taste, and add the Parmesan only if you wish. Serve immediately.

Serves 5 to 6

NOTE: Look for buckwheat noodles in a natural foods store if they are not sold in your supermarket. They can also be found in oriental groceries where they are known by the Japanese name, *soba*.

The olive purée comes in small jars. If you can't find it, try making your own by puréeing the strong-flavored Greek or Italian black olives in a food processor.

There is an added attraction to this unusual dish: the color is most unexpected, and the effect of the pale-brown pasta with its grainy, dark sauce against a white dinner plate is most elegant.

Spaghetti with Tuna and Capers

1 pound thin spaghetti
1 can (7 ounces) tuna packed in
   oil

juice of 1 large lemon
⅓ cup olive oil
2 tablespoons small capers

In a large saucepan bring about 3 quarts of salted water to a rolling boil. Add the spaghetti and cook for 5 to 6 minutes, or until al dente. Drain and run cold water over to prevent the spaghetti from continuing to cook.

In a large, warm bowl break up the tuna with a fork. In another bowl beat the lemon juice and oil with a whisk. Pour the spaghetti over the tuna and pour in the oil-lemon mixture.

If the capers are packed in brine, drain them; if they are packed in salt, rinse them. Scatter the capers over the spaghetti and toss very well. Serve immediately.

Serves 4 to 5

NOTE: This is one of the rare times when no Parmesan should be added. The tuna and lemon juice don't mix well with the cheese.

Pasta with Olive and Anchovy Sauce

1 pound peeled fresh or canned
   plum tomatoes
2 anchovy filets
1 cup Italian or Greek oil-cured
   black olives

½ cup virgin olive oil
1 clove garlic
½ pound pasta, preferably green

Chop the tomatoes coarsely. Chop the anchovies. Pit the olives and chop them finely.

Heat the olive oil in a large skillet over low heat. Add the tomatoes when the oil begins to get hot and mash them somewhat with a wooden spoon. Add the anchovies and garlic. When the liquid from the tomatoes has almost evaporated, add the olives and remove the garlic clove.

Bring a large pot of water to a boil and add the pasta. Cook until al dente, then drain well.

Heat a bowl and then pour the sauce into it. Add the pasta and toss.

Serves 4

NOTE: For some reason this sauce seems most successful with green pasta; it certainly looks great.

To avoid pitting the oily black olives, substitute a jar of finely chopped olives (almost puréed), sold in most specialty food shops.

Pasta with Uncooked Tomato Sauce

2 large ripe tomatoes
3 tablespoons virgin olive oil
salt (optional)
½ teaspoon freshly ground black
   pepper
½ pound spaghetti or bucatini

2 heaping tablespoons finely
   chopped basil
2 tablespoons sweet butter
⅓ cup freshly grated Parmesan
   cheese

Peel and seed the tomatoes. Chop them finely but do not use a food processor; there should be little "biteable" chunks of tomatoes. Place the tomatoes in a bowl and add the oil, salt, and pepper. Cover and let the bowl stand for a couple of hours.

Cook the pasta until al dente. While it is cooking, add the basil to the tomatoes and stir.

Heat a shallow bowl or a deep platter and place the butter in the center. Drain the pasta and pour it over the butter. Toss and add the sauce, mixing well and rapidly. Sprinkle the Parmesan over the top (or serve separately).

Serves 4 to 5

Basic Polenta

8 cups water
1 tablespoon coarse salt

2 cups coarse cornmeal
kettle of boiling water in reserve

Bring the 8 cups of water to a boil in a large, well-balanced saucepan. Add the salt.

Turn the heat down somewhat and, holding a long wooden spoon in one hand, the cup with the cornmeal in the other, start pouring the cornmeal into the water in a very fine stream, stirring constantly to avoid lumps. The water must remain at a steady simmer. If the mush seems to thicken too fast, add a little boiling water. The exact amount of water can't be given because some cornmeal will thicken faster than others. The proportions given are usually just right.

When all the cornmeal has been absorbed and the mixture is free of lumps, continue to simmer and stir; as the polenta thickens it will become more difficult to stir. Be careful not to stand too close to the saucepan as polenta "spits." The classic stirring time is 40 minutes, but see note.

The polenta is done when it no longer clings to the sides of the saucepan. You may now serve it as is, with a lump of fresh butter on top, or with both butter and a little Parmesan. You may also top the polenta with tomato sauce.

Serves 6 to 8

NOTE: Now that pasta and pizza are as familiar as apple pie in the United States, we may be adding another Italian specialty to our culinary repertoire. A marvelous alternative to rice, noodles, or potatoes is beginning to appear on the menus of some excellent restaurants. It is made of cornmeal and known as *polenta* in Italian. The meal is like that used in the American South, only coarsely ground. And there the similarity ends.

Polenta can be treated in many different ways, but the basic preparation is always the same. It is time-consuming and requires a strong right arm and a steady left hand—which is the reason many cooks shy away from it. But a new utensil imported from the Friuli, one of the northernmost provinces of Italy where polenta is a staple, is changing all that.

It is a large copper saucepan equipped with a metal dasher in the shape of an oversized comb. Start cooking the cornmeal as in the preceding recipe, but as soon as the mush is smooth—which shouldn't take more than 5 minutes—insert the dasher in the mush, plug the cord into the nearest outlet, and go about your business. Forty minutes later, you have perfect polenta without the slightest effort on your part.

■

Cheese Topped with Polenta

*6 slices soft, mild-flavored
   cheese (Mascarpone,
   Taleggio, or Gorgonzola), at
   room temperature*

*4 cups polenta (cooked
   according to preceding recipe)
6 teaspoons butter (optional)*

Place a slice of cheese on each of 6 medium-sized serving dishes. Divide the hot polenta over the slices and top each with a teaspoon of butter, if desired.

Serves 6

NOTE: You may arrange the cheese on the plates ahead of time. While the cornmeal is bubbling in its saucepan (assuming you have an assistant, mechanical or otherwise), you can serve drinks without worrying about your first course. While your guests sit down, you disappear into the kitchen for a couple of minutes, spoon the polenta over the cheese, and serve. You can pass the butter for those who want it.

SPECIALTY SALADS

I adore salads and find as many chances as I can to serve them to my guests. They are gathered together in this chapter to show just how versatile salads are. I've included simple vegetable salads, such as the Knob Celery Slivers with Mustard Mayonnaise as well as a variety of chicken salads, all of which could easily be the basis for an entire meal. Many are wonderful appetizers when served in small portions.

Carrot and Olive Salad

5 or 6 medium carrots
juice of 1 lemon
1 teaspoon sea salt
1 teaspoon freshly ground white
   pepper
⅓ cup olive oil

10 Greek, Italian, or Moroccan
   oil-cured olives
6 leaves Boston lettuce
1 small bunch fresh Italian
   parsley

Buy very tender young carrots. Large, mature carrots tend to have tough cores. Scrape the carrots and rinse them. Pat dry and grate, using the medium-sized holes on an old-fashioned grater. A food processor can't do the job properly and, fortunately, carrots are easy to grate. (Stop before you get to your knuckles or nails.)

Place the carrots in a bowl and add the lemon juice, salt, pepper, and oil. Toss very well. Let stand for a little while to give the salt a chance to dissolve.

Pit the olives and chop them fairly fine.

Place a lettuce leaf on each of 6 small plates. Heap some of the carrots in the hollow of the leaf. Sprinkle a bit of chopped olives on top. Just before serving, chop the parsley leaves very fine and sprinkle a little on each portion.

Serves 6

NOTE: I suggest white pepper instead of black only for aesthetic reasons. Tiny flecks of black pepper throughout the carrots would detract from the garnish of black olives.

I give you the choice of 3 kinds of olives: at least one should be available no matter where you live. The only olive to avoid is the glossy California kind. Sorry, no taste!

This salad is also appropriate for a buffet, and looks particularly attractive heaped in a glass bowl.

Knob Celery Slivers with Mustard Mayonnaise

1 large celery knob (celeriac)
juice of ½ lemon
½ cup mayonnaise, preferably
  homemade (page 194)

1 tablespoon Dijon mustard
1 teaspoon capers (optional)

Trim and peel the knob as in the recipe for Purée of Knob Celery on page 236. Slice it as thin as possible, ¼ inch at most. This can be done with a food processor. Julienne the slices to the thickness of emaciated French fries. Drop the sticks in a bowl of cold water mixed with lemon juice to prevent their darkening. You may keep them in the water for several hours.

When ready to prepare your salad, drain the sticks and dry well on paper towels. Mix the mayonnaise with the mustard and toss the mixture with the celery. Refrigerated, this salad will keep overnight. If you wish to add the capers, chop them fine and sprinkle over the salad at the last moment.

Serves 4

Green Bean Salad with Balsamic Vinegar Dressing

1 pound fresh green beans *salt to taste*
⅓ cup olive oil *2 small scallions*
4 tablespoons balsamic vinegar
  (aceto balsamico)

Wash the beans and snip off the tail ends; if they are very long, break them in half. Boil in plenty of lightly salted water until they are done but not soft. Rinse them under cold water to prevent them from continuing to cook.

In a serving bowl (glass, porcelain, or earthenware) combine the oil with the balsamic vinegar and mix well with a wire whisk. Drop the beans into the dressing and toss for a couple of minutes. All the beans should be evenly coated. Add salt to taste.

Cut off the roots and the green tops from the scallions. Chop the white part very fine and scatter over the beans before serving.

Serves 4

NOTE: Balsamic vinegar is a newcomer to this country and one that has taken the country by a storm. I find that it is available in the West as well as in the East and in points between. It is interesting that it is also a relative newcomer in its native Italy, where it is now very popular. Since it is new there too, it can't be found anywhere in the classic cuisine of the country.

As for the beans, I say "snip off the tail ends" advisedly. At a recent gathering of food enthusiasts we agreed that the tender little tip should not be snipped off at all. It is edible and looks pretty.

Egg, Endive, and Pear Salad

4 large eggs
1 lemon
4 firm ripe pears

6 medium Belgian endives
¼ cup light oil
freshly ground white pepper

Bring water to a boil in a saucepan. With a large spoon gently add the eggs, one by one. Count from the moment the water starts boiling again and let the eggs simmer rapidly for 12 minutes. They will be hard but the yolk won't have a dark rim. Transfer the eggs to cold water. Let cool, then peel them carefully. For this dish it is important that they look good. Using an egg slicer or a very sharp knife, cut them into thin rounds.

Squeeze the lemon and reserve the skin. Carefully peel the pears and rub with the inside of the lemon peels to prevent discoloring. Cut the pears in half lengthwise and remove the core and the slightly woody part from the center. Cut the pears into thin slices.

Wash and trim the endives, discarding any wilted leaves, and cut into pieces about 1 to 1½ inches square.

Mix the lemon juice with the oil until well amalgamated.

Place the eggs, endives, and pears in a bowl. Pour the oil and lemon juice mixture over them and toss gently. Grind the desired amount of pepper over the salad and toss again very lightly.

Serves 6

NOTE: This salad may be served on individual plates. In that case, the pepper should be grated over each portion. Personally I would not use salt on this dish. On the other hand, there is no law against it.

Melon Salad with Rum

1 large ripe cantaloupe
1 medium honeydew or
   Cranshaw melon
3 tablespoons white rum
3 tablespoons white wine
   vinegar

3 tablespoons olive oil
freshly ground black pepper to
   taste
lime wedges

Cut the melons in half and remove the seeds. Peel them and cut into thin slices, holding them over a bowl to catch all their juices as you work. Toss the pieces gently to combine. Refrigerate. Place the rum, vinegar, melon juices, and olive oil in a small bowl and mix well.

Divide the melon slices among 6 small plates. When ready to serve, pour the dressing over the slices and add the pepper at the last minute. Serve chilled, with lime wedges on the side.

Serves 6

NOTE: The melons may be sliced ahead of time and chilled, and the dressing added just before serving. The olive oil for the dressing should be the pale, refined kind; a heavy green oil would add too much flavor. Or use hazelnut oil—the lightest of all.

Red Cabbage with Goat Cheese

½ pound red cabbage, shredded
6 tablespoons virgin olive oil

1 cup crumbled goat (chèvre)
cheese, such as Montrachet
or Bucheron

Divide the cabbage between 2 plates and pour half the oil over each. Set aside.

Heat water in a large pot and put a plate on top. Place the goat cheese on the plate and cover it. As the water boils, the cheese will get warm.

When ready to serve, remove the cover, break up the cheese with a fork, scatter it over the cabbage, and serve.

Serves 2

NOTE: Whoever reads this book must by now have realized that I am a salad maniac. This particular combination was served me in a new little restaurant in New York City. I loved it. But one isn't always in the mood for shredded cabbage, so I tried it with watercress and found it delicious. For both versions I didn't add either salt or vinegar; they didn't seem to need them.

Mushroom, Celery, Parmesan, and Truffle Salad

12 medium mushroom caps
3 or 4 stalks celery from the
   heart
½ cup very thin slivers
   Parmesan cheese
juice of ½ lemon

⅓ cup virgin olive oil
freshly ground black pepper to
   taste
1 fresh white truffle, about the
   size of a walnut

The mushroom caps should be well shaped and without blemishes. Wipe them with a damp cloth and slice as thin as possible.

Chop the tender little stalks of celery medium-fine.

Place the mushrooms, celery, and Parmesan slivers in a glass or porcelain bowl. Pour the lemon juice over them, add the olive oil and pepper, and toss gently.

Scrape the truffle gently with a small, very sharp knife and remove any traces of sand from the little nooks with the point of the knife or a soft brush. Wipe the truffle with a damp cloth. Holding it over the bowl, shave the truffle over the other ingredients. Don't toss.

Serves 4

Tomato and Feta Cheese Salad

3 very large ripe tomatoes
coarse salt
½ teaspoon fresh tarragon
about ½ teaspoon fresh or dried
  oregano

3 tablespoons aceto balsamico
  (see note)
½ cup crumbled feta cheese
½ cup coarsely chopped black
  olives

Dip the tomatoes into boiling water and peel them. Slice the tomatoes fairly thin, place them on a platter, and sprinkle with coarse salt. Let stand for at least 30 minutes.

Pour off the juices from the tomatoes and arrange them on a platter, overlapping slightly. Sprinkle the tarragon and oregano over them. Don't overdo the oregano; it can be an overpowering herb. Pour the *aceto balsamico* over the tomatoes and allow it to sink in, then sprinkle with the feta and the chopped olives. Let stand in a cool place before serving.

Serves 6

NOTE: Aceto balsamico, or balsamic vinegar, is a newcomer to these shores. It is an herbed wine vinegar with 6 percent acidity, which is 1 percent more than the average wine vinegar. Its flavor, however, is not sharp, but quite subtle and unique. It is a complete condiment that doesn't require oil, particularly when it is combined with olives and feta, as it is here.

If you can't acquire a bottle of *aceto balsamico*, you might improvise: place a pinch of dry mustard in a bowl, add 1 tablespoon wine vinegar, and stir well to dissolve the mustard. Add 2 to 3 tablespoons olive oil, mix well, and pour the dressing over the tomatoes.

The olives should be very flavorful. I find Italian olives best for this salad. If you can find the ones called Olive di Gaeta, buy them. They are easily recognizable; the ends are pointed, rather than round.

Buckwheat-Cucumber Salad

2 cups broth or water   ½ cup minced parsley
1 cup buckwheat   1 tablespoon wine vinegar
1 small cucumber   ⅓ cup olive oil

Bring broth or water to a boil in a saucepan as you would for rice. Add the buckwheat and cook over high heat until it is al dente, meaning firm. About 10 minutes. Don't overcook.

Drain well and let cool completely.

Peel and seed the cucumber and chop very fine. If you have a food processor cut the cucumber into 3 or 4 pieces and, using the sharp blade, turn the motor on and off a couple of times until the cucumber is chopped fine, but not purée. The parsley may also be minced very finely in the food processor.

Add the cucumber and parsley to the buckwheat. Add the vinegar and toss. Add the olive oil, toss, and taste. Your palate might demand a little more vinegar.

Let stand a while, but toss again just before serving.

Serves 4

NOTE: The buckwheat should be the type you buy in natural foods stores. The kind you buy in boxes in supermarkets gets mushy when you boil it. It's alright as a breakfast cereal but not for salads, when you want the kernels to stay separate.

Minestrone, page 218

Zesty Rice Salad

2 cups long-grain rice
salt to taste
1 tablespoon Dijon-style
    mustard
½ cup mayonnaise, preferably
    homemade (page 194)

6 hard-cooked eggs
10 thin slices prosciutto or
    cooked ham
1 tablespoon capers

Bring about 3 quarts of water to a strong boil in a large saucepan, add the salt, and then the rice. Cook, stirring frequently, over high heat for about 15 minutes, or until the rice is done, al dente. Drain the rice into a colander and replace the saucepan on the burner, heat turned off. Place the colander on top of the saucepan and fluff the rice lightly with a fork. There will be enough heat left to dry the rice. Transfer the rice to a deep bowl and let cool.

Mix the mustard with the mayonnaise and add to the rice, stirring well to coat every grain.

Chop the eggs coarse and add to the rice. Chop the prosciutto or cooked ham. The pieces should be fairly coarse. Add the prosciutto to the rice and mix well. Before serving, sprinkle the capers over the top.

This may be prepared well ahead of time, but not so far ahead that it must be refrigerated.

Serves 6 to 8

NOTE: If you would like a richer salad, increase the amount of mayonnaise or add 3 tablespoons of olive or hazelnut oil.

Curried Shrimp and Rice Salad

1 tablespoon salt
2 cups long-grain rice
½ cup mayonnaise, preferably
   homemade (page 194)

15 large shrimp or 25 small
   shrimp, cleaned, deveined,
   and boiled
2 tablespoons curry powder
1 medium ripe cantaloupe

Bring about 3 quarts of water to a strong boil in a large saucepan, add the salt, and then the rice. Cook, stirring frequently, over high heat for about 15 minutes, or until the rice is done but still firm, or al dente.

Drain the rice in a colander and replace the saucepan on the burner, heat turned off. Place the colander on top of the saucepan and fluff the rice lightly with a fork. There should be enough heat left to dry the rice. Place it in a deep bowl and let cool.

Add the mayonnaise and mix well. If you are using large shrimp, cut them in half. If they are small, leave them whole. Add the shrimp and curry powder to the rice, mix well, and taste. Curry powder varies in strength and you might want a little more.

Cut the cantaloupe in half, remove the seeds, and with the appropriate gadget, cut it into balls. Add the melon to the rice just before serving.

Serves 6

NOTE: This is an unusual combination, and might sound funny, but it is delicious. The cantaloupe must be in season; otherwise it tastes of nothing. It is also a most attractive dish.

Laura's Rice and Seafood Salad

2 tablespoons olive oil
1 pound scallops, bay or sea
1 pound small shrimp, cooked
   and peeled
6 cups cooked long-grain rice
   (al dente)
½ cup pitted and coarsely
   chopped oil-cured black olives

3 tablespoons small capers (see
   note)
½ cup virgin olive oil
4 tablespoons red wine vinegar
salt and freshly ground black
   pepper to taste
⅓ cup finely chopped sweet basil

Heat 2 tablespoons olive oil in a skillet. If the scallops are small bay scallops, add them to the oil and sauté for a couple of minutes. If they are large sea scallops, cut them in half before sautéeing them. Set aside to cool slightly.

Cut the shrimp in half. Place the rice in a salad bowl (glass or porcelain) and add the seafood, olives, and capers.

In another bowl, use a wire whisk to beat the oil and the vinegar together with the salt and the pepper. Pour the mixture over the rice and the seafood and toss. Sprinkle the basil over the salad at the last moment and toss again gently. Don't chill; serve at room temperature.

Serves 6 to 8

NOTE: Capers come either bottled in vinegar or cured in salt. If you use the first type, pour off the vinegar and use the capers as they are. If the capers are preserved in salt, rinse before using.

Arugula and Prosciutto Salad

1 bunch arugula
⅓ cup olive oil
3 tablespoons red wine vinegar
    (optional)

2 slices lean prosciutto
⅓ cup slivered Parmesan cheese

Wash the arugula and snip off the tips of the stems if they look tough. Place in a salad bowl and add the oil and the vinegar, if desired. I feel that the sharpness of the arugula needs no vinegar. Toss.

Remove the fat from the edges of the prosciutto and chop the meat very coarsely. You should have pieces of prosciutto, not scraps. Add to the salad.

There is a gadget to cut slivers off your Parmesan. If you don't have one, a very sharp small knife will do. Scatter the slivers over the salad and serve without further tossing, which would break up the cheese.

Serves 2

NOTE: Arugula is a sharp green that is at its best in the spring and early summer. It has become so popular that it is grown in hothouses and is sometimes available in winter but then it has much less taste.

If arugula is not available, you might try watercress for a different result. Pour the oil over it just before serving because watercress wilts very quickly.

Tuna and Pepper Relish

1 cup canned tuna, loosely
   packed
3 small tender stalks celery
½ green pepper

½ sweet red pepper
olive oil to taste
vinegar to taste
freshly ground pepper (optional)

Break up the tuna with a fork. There should be no chunks, only small bits.

Chop the celery and the peppers medium-fine. They should be crunchy.

Mix the tuna with the vegetables and taste the mixture before you add oil and vinegar. The quantity will depend on how much oil there is in the tuna. Add some freshly ground pepper if you like a very piquant flavor.

Toss well and refrigerate for several hours before serving.

Serves 4

Scallops and Grapefruit Salad

1 pound large sea scallops
juice of 1 lime
2 bunches watercress, rinsed
*   and trimmed*

24 grapefruit sections
pepper to taste
½ cup thin mayonnaise
*   (page 194)*

Wash the scallops under cold running water and dry on a towel. Hold a scallop in your hand and, with a very sharp knife, cut it in half horizontally. This operation is surprisingly easy. If the scallop is very thick, cut it into 3 slices. (You will need about 10 scallop slices per serving.) Place the rounds on a platter and pour the lime juice over them. Let stand for at least 1 hour.

Bring a small saucepan of water to a rolling boil. Cook the scallop in this way: place 2 or 3 scallop rounds on a slotted spoon and immerse carefully in the boiling water for about 30 seconds. Do not let the scallops slip off the spoon. Drain the rounds on a paper towel. When they are cool enough to handle, arrange them on 6 individual plates as follows: place some watercress in the center of each plate and arrange alternate groups of a few rounds and a few grapefruit sections around the cress. Grind some fresh pepper over the scallops and coat them very lightly with mayonnaise. Thin the mayonnaise, if necessary, with a little virgin olive oil. Refrigerate and serve chilled, but not ice cold.

Serves 6

Green Beans, Avocado, and Chicken Salad

2 whole chicken breasts, with
   bones
1 pound small green beans
⅓ cup olive oil
2 ripe avocados
⅓ cup pignoli or pinenuts
   (optional)

1 teaspoon Dijon-style mustard
1 cup thin homemade
   mayonnaise (page 194)
freshly ground pepper to taste
salt (optional)

Poach and then remove skin and bone the chicken breasts. Pour off part of the broth (reserve for other use), leaving just enough broth in the saucepan to keep the breasts moist and warm. Place boned breasts back into saucepan.

Snip off the tail end of the green beans and wash them. Bring water to a boil in a saucepan and add the beans. Cook until firm but done; if the beans are small, 8 minutes is the exact cooking time. Drain and toss in a bowl with the oil.

Peel and cube the avocados, then scatter the cubes over the beans. If using the pignolis, scatter them over the vegetables.

Remove the chicken breasts from the warm broth and cut them into slivers, as thin as possible. Arrange the chicken over the mound of vegetables. Add the mustard to the mayonnaise, then pour the mayonnaise over the chicken in a thin stream. If desired, grind pepper over the salad and season to taste with salt.

Serves 6

NOTE: If you are not going to serve the salad immediately, place several lettuce leaves over it and then just remove them at the moment of serving. The leaves prevent the dressing from drying out.

Some markets now carry tiny French green beans. They are delicious, but frightfully expensive. An alternative is to use long beans, available in oriental markets; they are about 15 inches long so you must cut them to a desired length.

Cipriani's Chicken Salad

1 roasting chicken, about 3
   pounds
3 heads Belgian endive
10 leaves romaine lettuce

5 stalks celery (tender white
   stalks only)
1½ cups thin mayonnaise
   (page 194)

In a saucepan that should not be much larger than the chicken, stew the bird until tender, about 30 minutes. While it is cooling, chop the endive, lettuce, and celery as finely as possible.

Prepare the mayonnaise following the recipe on page 194, adding a touch of mustard and the juice of ½ lemon.

Using a bowl or a deep platter (porcelain or glass but not wood), make a bed of the vegetables at the bottom. When the chicken is cool enough to handle, remove the skin and coarsely shred the meat with your hands, being careful to remove dark veins or tendons. The pieces should be rather large. Place the chicken on top of the shredded vegetables and cover with the mayonnaise. Don't toss until the moment of serving.

Serves 4 to 5

NOTE: Cipriani was the founder of the famous Harry's Bar in Venice. He had three rules. Don't use ingredients out of season; they are expensive and have little taste. Don't waste food; be careful about the quantities you prepare, and if you should have leftovers, be imaginative in using them. Be aware of the appearance of food; you eat partly with your eyes.

It was the third rule that made him suggest to toss the chicken salad only at the moment of serving it. It looks much better with the unbroken mayonnaise on top.

I have a passion for a good chicken salad. At times I add ½ cup fine slivers of Swiss cheese to the greens and place the chicken pieces on top. I also add freshly ground pepper, but—keeping Cipriani in mind—never on top of the pristine mayonnaise; it would no longer be pristine! I either add the pepper to the greens or I hand the peppermill to each person to add individually.

Chicken Salad with Bourbon

1 roasting chicken, about 2½ to
   3 pounds
1 large carrot
2 stalks celery
1 medium turnip
2 firm large apples

½ lemon
3 tablespoons Worcestershire
   sauce (see note)
1 cup mayonnaise, preferably
   homemade
3 tablespoons bourbon (see note)

Remove the wing tips from the chicken; wash chicken inside and outside. Place it in a saucepan that is only big enough to hold the chicken and the vegetables.

Clean the vegetables and place them on top and around the chicken. Cover with water and simmer over medium heat for about 30 minutes or until the chicken is tender.

Remove chicken from the broth, and allow to cool: Don't discard the broth and the vegetables; it is the basis for a very good soup.

When the chicken is cool enough to handle, remove the skin, bone, and cut the meat into large chunks; place chicken in a shallow bowl. (Personally I don't like to cut it into small bits; it makes the salad look storebought.)

Core and peel the apples. Before cutting them into cubes, rub them with the lemon half to prevent them from turning brown. Cube apples and add them to the chicken.

Blend together the Worcestershire with the mayonnaise. Add the bourbon and mix well. Spoon the dressing over the chicken and toss. Serve at room temperature.

Serves 4 to 5

NOTE: The quantities here are my own personal choice for seasoning. You might want to add more, or less, Worcestershire and bourbon. In any case, you don't need salt and pepper; the Worcestershire takes their place.

This salad can be a first course or a main course, and looks beautiful on a buffet.

Mayonnaise

2 large eggs
pinch of salt
pinch of pepper

1 teaspoon dry mustard
  (optional)
1 tablespoon lemon juice
1½ cups olive oil

Break the eggs into the bowl of a food processor. Add the salt, pepper, mustard, and lemon juice and, using the steel blade, run the processor for a few seconds. Place the feed tube over the bowl and run the motor while adding the oil through the tube drop by drop. Don't stop the motor until the mixture is beginning to thicken.

Test the mixture and, if it is beginning to get creamy, continue to process but add the remaining oil in a constant, very thin stream. When all the oil is absorbed the mayonnaise should have the desired thickness.

Yields approximately 2 cups

NOTE: By using the whole eggs, you will get a lighter mayonnaise, both in texture and in color. I find, however, that I am not very successful using the whole eggs when I make the mayonnaise by hand, using a wire whisk or even a wooden spoon. In that case using only the yolks works better.

I include this recipe for mayonnaise because so many recipes in my book call for homemade mayonnaise. You could also use your favorite recipe.

MAIN COURSES

Main courses are also your main entertaining problem, not because they are necessarily the most complicated or the most costly part of the meal, but because they are the most important. The rest—appetizer, first course, dessert—should be built around them. If the main course is a flop, your dinner can't be a success. And sometimes a small oversight can spoil it.

I recently went to a dinner. The first course was delicious, the table beautifully set. The main course was a rolled roast of veal. It looked fine, but whoever was in the kitchen had forgotten to remove the string that held the roast. And there was a lot of string. The cook must have been worried that the meat might un-roll. Somehow the roast got sliced but the conversation was not much; we were all trying to remove pieces of string from our teeth as gracefully as possible.

Happenings like this are, of course, the exception, not the rule. There is one rule that applies: be careful with your food to the last detail. Be sure you remove the strings from meat, bones from chickens that are supposed to be boneless, and bones from fish that should be boneless filets.

Shrimps with Peppers and Feta

3 pounds raw shrimp in the shell
juice of 1 lime
2 large green peppers
4 tablespoons olive oil
1 scallion, chopped fine

1 clove garlic
1 can (15 ounces) tomato purée
1 cup dry white wine
1 tablespoon vodka (optional)
½ pound feta cheese

Shell the shrimp and devein if you wish. (In Europe they don't bother.) Pour the lime juice over the shrimp and set aside to marinate.

Cut the peppers in half lengthwise, remove the seeds, then cut the peppers into strips about ½ inch wide.

Heat 2 tablespoons of the oil in a skillet and add the scallion, peppers, and the whole garlic clove. When the peppers are wilted but not brown, remove the garlic and add the tomato purée and the wine. Let simmer, uncovered for 20 minutes.

Heat the remaining oil in another skillet and sauté the shrimp. As soon as they are pink, add them to the sauce and transfer the mixture to a heatproof casserole. Add the vodka if desired and let simmer very gently over very low heat for another 10 minutes. Crumble the feta and scatter over the surface of the dish. Cover and let simmer for another 2 or 3 minutes to give the feta a chance to melt. Total cooking time is 30 to 35 minutes. Serve in the casserole.

Serves 6

NOTE: This dish is a financial investment but it is worth it. I first tasted it at the house of a bachelor friend of mine who is a great cook. It was my birthday, and the dish was indeed a great present. My friend used Pernod, and you may use that instead of vodka if you like the flavor of anise. Or, use ouzo if you want to be really Greek.

The dish may be prepared an hour or so before serving. Just make sure it is hot when it comes to the table. Serve it with steamed rice and follow with a light dessert.

Poached Whole Fish

1 striped bass or red snapper, about 5 pounds	*2 stalks celery*
1 carrot	*2 bay leaves*
	1 teaspoon peppercorns

To poach fish successfully, you really should have a fish poacher. It is well worth the investment as it comes in handy for several other uses.

Wash the fish under cold running water. Don't remove either the head or the tail. If it is a little too long for your poacher, trim the tail as little as possible, but never remove the head! Place the carrot, celery, bay leaves, and peppercorns on the tray in the poacher. Cut the lemon in half and add. Place the fish on top of the vegetables and add water until the fish is barely submerged. Place the poacher over very low heat and bring the water to a simmer as slowly as possible. By the time it actually boils the fish should be almost done. Test it with a fork; when it flakes easily, it is done. If you are in doubt, lift it out on its tray, place it briefly on a platter, and look inside, right under the head where the fish is thickest. If you see no trace of blood, the fish is done.

Serves 6 to 8

NOTE: If you plan to serve the fish warm, it can stay in the water for a little while. Remove it just before bringing it to the table. If you plan to serve it at room temperature, place it on a platter and cover with plastic wrap until the time comes to decorate it. Place lots of parsley around the head and under the tail, place lemon wedges and small boiled potatoes around it for a spectacular dish.

Serve accompanied with buttered green beans.

Ibrahim's Fish with Green Sauce

1 onion
3 bay leaves
1 teaspoon peppercorns
2 pounds striped bass filets
2 pounds flounder filets or
*   similar fish*
1 carrot

1¼ cups olive oil
4 average bunches Italian
*   parsley*
¾ cup milk
2 teaspoons cornstarch
½ cup ground unsalted peanuts

Place the vegetables, bay leaves, and peppercorns on the bottom of a fish poacher. Wash the fish filets and place them on the tray of the poacher. Add water until the fish is barely covered. Over very low heat, bring the water to a slow boil. When it starts boiling, the fish should be almost done. Test with a fork and if it flakes easily, turn off the heat and allow the fish to cool in its liquid.

Remove the fish from the liquid and remove stray bones, if any. Flake it, mixing the bass and the flounder together. Pour ½ cup of the oil over the fish and, pressing gently with your hands, place the fish on a serving platter, patting it into the approximate shape of a fish.

Wash the parsley and dry it on a paper towel. Remove the stems. Place the leaves in a food processor and, using the sharp blade, chop them as fine as possible. There should be 1 cup of rough pureé.

Place the parsley in a blender and add the milk and the remaining oil. Blend until smooth.

Heat about 2 tablespoons water in a saucepan and add the cornstarch. Dissolve and bring briefly to a boil. Let cool and add to the parsley mixture. Blend. Add the peanuts and blend until the sauce is smooth; it should have the consistency of a thick mayonnaise.

Cover the fish with most of the sauce, leaving a little sauce to be added at the last moment. Let the dish stand for at least 30 minutes before serving, then serve at room temperature.

Serves 6

NOTE: A fascinating Italian diplomat, stationed in this country, has an impressive houseman named Ibrahim, who is also a great cook. At a recent buffet supper there was one special dish that had everyone overeating and trying to guess what they were eating. I asked for the recipe and was told that it was fish covered with an Arabic sauce. When his boss asked Ibrahim to give me the recipe, he suddenly didn't speak enough English or Italian to do so. "Then you will prepare the sauce in the presence of the lady," said his boss. At this threat Ibrahim rediscovered his English. The directions he gave me were, however, incomplete and it took many tests before I came up with a sauce that tastes and looks like his.

Ibrahim, whose tastes seem to run to the surrealistic, had placed an empty fish head at one end of the dish and a fish tail at the other. I prefer to place half a lemon, cut lengthwise, at the head and a few sprigs of parsley at the tail. Either way it's sensational.

Swordfish with Peas

1 swordfish steak, about 1
   pound
½ cup olive oil
1 clove garlic
salt and pepper to taste

1 cup thick tomato juice
1 cup shelled fresh peas
1 teaspoon finely chopped
   parsley

Rinse the fish and pat dry with paper towels.

Heat the oil in a large skillet over medium heat and add the whole garlic clove. Add the swordfish steak and allow it to brown on one side; turn it with a spatula and sprinkle with salt and pepper. Remove the garlic and add the tomato juice. Bring to a boil, lower heat, and simmer gently until the fish flakes easily, about 15 to 20 minutes. The skin should be crisp.

Remove the fish to a warm platter, add the peas to the skillet, and cook until tender. Cooking time depends on the size of the peas. When they are done, carefully return the fish to the skillet and cook 1 minute longer.

Place the fish on a platter, pour the peas and sauce over it, and sprinkle with parsley.

If you wish, you may cut the fish into strips before serving.

Serves 2 to 3

NOTE: No accompanying vegetable other than boiled potatoes is needed with this dish. Nor should a salad be served with it as raw oil and fried oil don't go together.

Codfish Baked in Milk

1 to 1½ pounds dried salt cod
5 cups milk
1 tablespoon unsalted butter

1 medium white onion
4 large potatoes

Place the dried cod in a large bowl and cover with a mixture of 1 cup of the milk and 1 cup water. Let soak for a couple of hours, then pour off the liquid and replace it with fresh cold water. No need to add more milk. Let soak overnight. Change the water at least once more before cooking the fish.

Remove the skin and bones and cut the cod into bite-sized or slightly larger pieces.

Preheat the oven to 300°.

Butter an ovenproof dish, preferably rectangular or oval and fairly deep. In it, layer the fish. Cut the onion into very thin slices and layer them over the fish. Peel and slice the potatoes and layer them on top of the onion. Pour the 4 cups of milk over all and bake for 1 hour to 1 hour and 30 minutes, or until the fish flakes easily with a fork.

Serves 6

NOTE: Salted codfish is a greatly misunderstood creature. Like many people, I used to be happy to eat it in someone else's home or in a restaurant. But prepare it in my own kitchen—and live with the smell? Never! I have since learned that, properly soaked in clear water, dried codfish does not smell. It is lean and delicious, much easier to clean up afterwards than some rich, oily fish, and it costs a lot less.

Poached Chicken with Vegetables

1 roasting chicken, about 3 to
   3½ pounds
salt
2 leeks
2 or 3 carrots

2 or 3 white turnips
¼ head cabbage
freshly ground pepper to taste
   (optional)
water or broth

Wash the chicken inside and out. Remove the wing tips and the tail. Choose a saucepan in which the chicken will fit snugly. Fill the pan just halfway with water or broth and add salt to taste. Bring to a boil and add the chicken. It should be covered with the liquid but not submerged. Clean the vegetables and place them over and around the chicken. Lower the heat, cover the pan, and let simmer for about 35 to 45 minutes, depending on the age and size of the chicken. Test with a fork for doneness by piercing the skin near the thigh. The liquid that oozes out should have no trace of pink.

Leave the chicken in its broth until serving time. Remove it to a platter, sprinkle with pepper if you wish, place the vegetables around it, and serve.

Serves 4 to 6

NOTE: Some people feel that only a hen should be used for this method of cooking a chicken. If they want a very good broth, they are right. If they want a tender, juicy chicken, they are wrong. A hen will be tough no matter how long you boil it. There is an Italian saying: *"Gallina vecchia fa buon brodo,"* meaning, "an old hen makes good soup." Right. But that is all it does.

As for the vegetables, you may want to use cauliflower instead of cabbage, increase the leeks, or leave them out. It's a question of taste. A couple of potatoes would do no harm. Serve with one of the following horseradish sauces.

Horseradish Sauce

1 root horseradish,
approximately ½ pound
½ cup heavy cream
2 tablespoons granulated sugar

2 tablespoons bread crumbs,
approximately
4 tablespoons distilled white
vinegar, approximately

Scrape or peel the horseradish and grate it with a hand grater, using the next-to-largest openings. Since you won't be able to grate the root to the very end and as quite a bit gets lost when you peel it, you will have quite a bit less than ½ pound grated; you need at least 1 cup for the sauce.

Place the grated horseradish in a bowl and add the cream. Mix and then add the sugar and the bread crumbs until the sauce is the desired consistency and with the desired tartness.

Serves 4 to 6

NOTE: For another type of horseradish sauce, peel and grate the horseradish root as above. Peel and grate also 1 large tart apple and add the apple to the horseradish. Add the bread crumbs and 2 or 3 tablespoons of balsamic vinegar until you have the desired consistency. Omit the sugar and distilled vinegar.

Both recipes come from Alto Adige, the northernmost region of Italy near the Austrian border. The second, however, is a modern variation on the classic because balsamic vinegar doesn't exist in the classic cuisine. These sauces are excellent with boiled chicken, as indicated in the previous recipe, or with boiled meats, both hot and cold. The sauce may be prepared ahead of time, bottled, and kept in the refrigerator.

Chicken with Mushrooms and Tomatoes

1 broiling chicken,
about 3 pounds
coarse salt
freshly ground black pepper
2 tablespoons oil
1 medium onion chopped fine
10 medium mushroom caps,
halved or quartered

1 sprig rosemary, or ½ teaspoon
dried
3 large ripe tomatoes, peeled
and chopped coarse
1 cup dry white wine
1 tablespoon finely chopped
parsley

Cut the chicken into serving pieces. Remove the chunks of fat near the tail and remove the tail too, unless you are particularly fond of it. Wash the chicken pieces and pat dry with a paper towel. Sprinkle with salt and pepper to taste. Heat the oil in a skillet large enough to accommodate the chicken pieces without crowding them. When the oil is hot, add the chicken pieces and brown lightly over high heat, turning frequently so they are golden on all sides.

When the chicken is golden, check the fat on the bottom of the skillet and pour off the excess. What is left should just coat the bottom of the skillet. Add the onion and the mushrooms and stir to distribute them all over the chicken. Stir in the rosemary and the tomatoes and cook, uncovered, over low heat for about 10 minutes. Stir occasionally and make sure the chicken does not stick to the bottom of the skillet. Pour the wine over the chicken and, with a wooden spoon, loosen the particles of skin and fat that might be clinging to the skillet. Cover with a tight-fitting lid, lower the heat, and allow to simmer gently for about 15 minutes.

Remove the lid. If there seems to be too much liquid (the tomatoes may shed a lot of juice), raise the heat and cook, uncovered, for another couple of minutes. The chicken should have some sauce, but not be drowning in it. Just before removing the skillet from the heat, add the parsley, sprinkling it all over the chicken. Remove to a serving platter and serve with steamed rice or boiled potatoes or even alone. It really is a complete dish.

Serves 6 to 8

NOTE: If you have an earthenware casserole that is heatproof, brown the chicken pieces in a skillet and then transfer them to the casserole. Complete the cooking and bring the dish to the table in the casserole. There is no need to serve it immediately. It can remain in the casserole for a couple of hours, provided you cover it and heat it briefly before serving.

Chicken and Mushroom Casserole

2 small chickens, about 2½
    pounds each
1 tablespoon unsalted butter
2 tablespoons oil
1 pound fresh mushrooms
4 medium carrots
4 stalks celery
2 scallions

2 tablespoons finely chopped
    rosemary, or 1 tablespoon
    dried
1 cup dry white wine
1 cup chicken broth
coarse salt to taste
freshly ground pepper to taste
2 tablespoons finely chopped
    parsley

Have the butcher cut the chickens into serving pieces unless you own fabulous shears that permit you to do it yourself.

Remove the wing tips, the tail, and the chunks of yellow fat and skin from the tail end. But don't take the skin off the other parts. Wash the chicken pieces and pat dry.

Melt the butter in a heatproof casserole or Dutch oven and add the oil. Add the chicken pieces a few at a time and brown lightly on all sides. Remove them to a platter.

Preheat the oven to 325°.

Clean the mushrooms, wiping them with a wet cloth. Leave the small ones whole and halve or quarter the large ones. Add them to the casserole and sauté them for 3 or 4 minutes.

Peel the carrots and cut them into pieces 1 inch long. Wash the celery and the scallions, cut them into bite-sized pieces, and add. Add the rosemary, stir, and return the chicken pieces to the vegetables. Add the wine and the broth. Add salt and pepper to taste.

Cover the casserole and bake 1 hour to 1 hour and 30 minutes or until the chicken pieces are tender. Test with a fork before removing from the oven. During the cooking time uncover the casserole every now and then; if there seems to be too much liquid, continue cooking uncovered. There should be some sauce surrounding the chicken, but the bird shouldn't be immersed.

Before serving, scatter the parsley over the surface.

Serves 6 to 8

NOTE: This is actually a whole meal—fowl and vegetables all in one—and will probably serve only 6. If you have a first course (I don't think you should), it will serve 8.

This dish may be prepared a couple of hours before serving and may be kept warm in a lukewarm oven. Just add the parsley at the last moment.

Chicken and Vegetable Casserole

3 large chicken breasts
3 tablespoons unsalted butter
about 7 tablespoons oil
6 medium mushroom caps
1 medium potato

3 small firm zucchini
1 cup chopped Chinese cabbage
2 large ripe tomatoes
1 teaspoon fresh rosemary, or
½ teaspoon dried

Flatten the chicken breasts slightly with a wooden mallet, or with a short handled metal one. Bone and cut in half. Remove the skin if you wish.

Melt the butter in a large skillet and add 3 tablespoons of the oil. When the mixture is hot add the chicken breasts and sauté, turning frequently until pale gold on both sides. Remove from skillet.

Wipe the mushroom caps with a wet towel and slice coarse. Sauté briefly over high heat in the skillet in which you cooked the chicken, then remove and reserve. Peel and slice the potato and sauté in the same skillet, adding a little oil as needed. Wash and slice the zucchini and add. Add the chopped Chinese cabbage. Dip the tomatoes into boiling water and peel. Cut into quarters and add to the skillet along with a little more oil. Sprinkle with rosemary and simmer until most of the liquid from the tomatoes is absorbed.

Preheat the oven to 325°.

Make a bed of half the vegetables in an ovenproof dish with a lid. Place the chicken breasts on the vegetables. Cover the chicken breasts with the reserved mushrooms. Cover the mushrooms with the rest of the vegetables. Add salt and pepper if desired.

Cover the dish and place it in the oven. After 30 minutes remove the lid; if there is too much liquid, continue cooking uncovered. If contents seem too dry, add a little broth but this is most unlikely. Total cooking time should be less than an hour, including the sautéing.

Serves 6

NOTE: This dish may be varied according to the season or to your own personal taste. If zucchini are not in season, they may be replaced with white turnips and carrots. If you like onions, an onion may be added. The tomatoes are a must, however, as is the potato.

The dish may be prepared ahead of time and kept warm. It does not require any additional vegetable, of course. If you wish, steamed rice may be served with it.

Roasted Lemon Chicken

1 medium roasting chicken,
   about 2½ pounds
freshly ground black pepper to
   taste

3 lemons
1 sprig fresh sage or ½ teaspoon
   dried
1 tablespoon unsalted butter

Preheat the oven to 375°.

Wash the chicken inside and out and pat dry. Sprinkle pepper into the cavity. Cut 1 lemon into quarters and place them inside the chicken. Tie the legs together. If fresh sage is used, break the sprig in half and place each half between a wing and the breast, then tie the wings to the breast. If dried sage is used, sprinkle it over the chicken.

Place the chicken in a roasting pan. Squeeze the 2 remaining lemons and pour the juice over the chicken. Place the pan in the oven. After about 30 minutes, rub the top and sides of the bird with butter. Turn the chicken on its side and roast for about 20 minutes, then turn it on its other side and roast for another 20 minutes. Exact cooking time depends on the size and age of the bird, but it will be about 1 hour and 15 minutes.

When the chicken is tender, place it on a warm platter, remove the strings and sage, and serve.

Serves 4 to 6

NOTE: Unless you like your food very salty, this lemony chicken doesn't require any salt at all. Serve the chicken with buttered green beans or boiled zucchini—both go well with the flavor of lemon. Wine, on the other hand, doesn't fare well and only a light dry white would be a suitable accompaniment.

Chicken Livers with Sage

1 pound chicken livers
3 tablespoons oil
coarse salt to taste

freshly ground pepper to taste
1 sprig of fresh sage or ½
teaspoon dried leaf sage

Wash the chicken livers under cold running water and dry thoroughly with paper towels. Carefully remove the white membranes. If there is any green color, the liver should be discarded; it could be caused by bile from the gall bladder, and it will make the dish bitter. Cut the livers in half.

Heat the oil in a skillet large enough to hold the livers without heaping them on top of each other. Add the livers and cook over fairly high heat, moving them around to keep from sticking and turning them over to brown. Add the sage, salt, and pepper. Cook the livers just until no blood is visible; don't allow them to get dry. This will take about 3 minutes. If using fresh sage, discard it before serving the livers on a bed of rice, cooked al dente.

Serves 4

NOTE: Chicken livers have the advantage of being cheap as well as delicious. They have the disadvantage of having to be cooked at the last minute and served immediately. Ah, but consider this: your guests are seated around the dining room table. You are standing before a chafing dish or a simple iron skillet, a plate with the livers next to you and the other ingredients on a tray nearby. If you want to add glamour to the whole operation, you may add a couple of tablespoons of cognac to livers while they are cooking. Within 3 minutes and with a touch of panache, you can serve up the livers and join your guests at the table.

Sautéed Turkey Cutlets

1 pound turkey breast cutlets
2 large eggs
3 tablespoons all purpose flour

3 tablespoons oil
coarse salt
freshly ground black pepper
lemon wedges

Place the cutlets in a plastic bag and flatten the end with a short metal mallet. Remove, wash and pat dry. Beat the eggs well in a shallow bowl. Spread the flour on a platter or on a paper towel.

Heat the oil in a large skillet. Dip the cutlets in the flour, 1 at a time. Shake off the excess flour and, using a fork, dip them in the egg and again in the flour. Place them in the hot oil a few at a time so they don't crowd each other. Sauté the cutlets for a minute or so on each side. When they are golden brown, transfer them to a warm platter. (The best way to heat a platter and keep it hot is to heat the oven and turn it off before you need it. Then place the platter in the oven; it will stay hot for quite a while and won't crack.)

Sprinkle sparingly with coarse salt and add a little freshly ground black pepper. Place lemon wedges around them and serve.

Serves 4

NOTE: These cutlets can be found in most meat markets. I find they taste good and are quickly and easily prepared. I like to serve them with sautéed, sliced mushrooms. I sauté the mushrooms in the same skillet; it makes life quite easy.

Herbed Meat Loaf

2 pounds very lean beef
    (preferably sirloin or filet)
salt (optional)
1½ teaspoons freshly ground
    black pepper

½ teaspoon oregano
1 egg
3 tablespoons very strong black
    coffee

Preheat the oven to 375°.

Place the meat in a large bowl and break it up with a fork. Using your hands, add the salt, if you wish, pepper, and oregano. With your fingertips, work the spices into the meat so that they get as evenly distributed as possible. Add the egg and work it into the meat.

Oil a large baking pan. Pick up the meat in one batch with both hands. Without pressing hard with your hands, shape the meat into a loaf. Be certain there are no cracks in the surface where juices could escape. Place the loaf in the oiled pan and smooth whatever cracks may appear. The surface of the loaf should be quite flat. With your thumb, make a couple of grooves into the surface and pour the coffee into them, immediately spreading it all over the meat.

Place the baking pan in the oven and cook 30 minutes for rare and 40 minutes for well done. Let stand for 30 minutes, then serve at room temperature.

Serves 6

NOTE: For a party I make two loaves: one rare and one well done. The rare version is described by my friends as "steak tartar with a crust." The coffee has actually only a cosmetic function. It gives the meat a nice glossy surface.

Flank Steak with Green Peppercorns

1 flank steak, about 1½ to 2
   pounds
½ cup olive or vegetable oil

½ cup dry red wine
1 tablespoon green peppercorns
coarse salt to taste

Place the flank steak in a deep platter.

Mix the oil and wine with a wire whisk until they are amalgamated.

Sprinkle half the peppercorns over the steak and press them into the meat as firmly as possible. Pour half of the marinade over the meat and let stand for 10 minutes. Turn the meat. Some peppercorns will fall off—just leave them in the marinade. Sprinkle the rest of the peppercorns over the other side of the meat and press them in. Pour the rest of the marinade over the meat and let stand for another 10 minutes.

Preheat the broiler. When it is very hot, transfer the meat to a broiler pan with some of the marinade and broil about 5 inches from the heat.

After 3 minutes turn the meat, add the rest of the marinade, and broil to desired doneness.

Cooking time depends on the thickness of the meat. Three minutes for each side should produce a medium-rare steak. Just before serving, sprinkle with coarse salt.

Serves 6

NOTE: Flank steak is a neglected cut. When I once asked for it in a fancy butcher shop, the butcher replied haughtily, "We don't carry that cut." Too bad for both him and his customers. Properly prepared, flank steak is a treat. It should be sliced on a slant, as is London broil.

Green peppercorns are available in most fancy groceries. They come packed in brine or in water and will last for a long time even after the jar has been opened, if kept refrigerated.

They are less sharp than the black or white peppercorns and lend themselves very well to all sorts of meat dishes. To help them penetrate the meat I sometimes tap them gently with a wooden mallet. This doesn't work too well with flank steak because of its texture. But even if they don't penetrate the meat, they still add fine flavor to the dish.

■

Beef Stew

2 pounds beef bottom round, cut into 1-inch cubes
2 tablespoons unsalted butter or lard
2 large, ripe tomatoes or 3 cups peeled canned tomatoes

1 cup dry red wine
boiling water
1 teaspoon paprika
salt to taste

Pat the meat dry. Heat the butter or lard in a skillet over high heat and add the meat. Quickly sear it on all sides, using tongs to turn the pieces.

Peel and seed the tomatoes, chop coarse, and add them to the meat. Reduce the heat and bring to a simmer. Add the wine and cover the skillet tightly. Let simmer for 10 minutes without uncovering. If, at that point, the liquid has evaporated too much, and the skillet is dry, add a little boiling water. Stir, cover, and continue to simmer, adding boiling water as necessary to maintain liquid in the pan.

After about 40 minutes add the paprika, taste for seasoning, and add salt. Test the meat with a fork. It should be done, but if it is not quite tender, continue to simmer covered until the fork pierces it easily. Don't overcook or the meat will disintegrate.

Serves 6

Mary's Meat Pie

4 tablespoons oil
1 medium onion
3 shallots
1 clove garlic (optional)
3 pounds lean ground beef
  (chuck or sirloin)
1 can (1 pound) tomato sauce or
  peeled tomatoes
1 teaspoon oregano

3 tablespoons Worcestershire
  sauce
2 cups dry red wine
½ pound fresh mushrooms
salt and pepper (optional)
2 cups Bisquick, approximately

Heat the oil in a large skillet. Peel the onion, shallots, and garlic, if you are using it, and add to the oil. Sauté until the onion is transparent but not brown. Add the meat and stir with a wooden spoon to break it up into small lumps.

When the meat is no longer pink, add the tomato sauce, oregano, Worcestershire, and wine and let simmer over medium heat, stirring every now and then.

Wipe the mushrooms with a wet cloth and remove any sand and dark spots. Slice the large mushrooms and halve the small ones. Add to the meat. Simmer, uncovered, for 1 hour, or until enough liquid is absorbed so that it barely covers the meat. The consistency should be that of a stew rather than a soup.

Taste and see if you want to add salt and pepper.

At this point you have a choice: you either make the pie the same day or you let the mixture stand for 1 day and then make the pie. It is actually tastier the next day.

Preheat the oven to 400°.

Prepare the Bisquick according to directions on the package, using milk for mixing. Depending on the size of your casserole or Dutch oven, you might need more Bisquick. Stop when the surface is covered.

Mary's Meat Pie

Transfer the meat mixture to an ovenproof casserole, preferably one of those large, brown, glazed earthenware ones that make a meat pie look mouth-watering. Spoon the dough over the surface with a large spoon, remembering that the Bisquick will both rise and expand. Place the dish in the oven, and bake for 30 to 40 minutes or until the top is golden.

Serves 8 to 10

NOTE: When I asked my friend Mary for this recipe I got a haphazard answer, to say the least. "How many mushrooms?"

"That depends on how I feel and how much mushrooms cost that day." But what really left me bemused was the Bisquick; I had never heard of a pie top that came out of a box. So I tried it. The dish is no great achievement of a gourmet cook but people love it and nothing could be simpler to make.

It's even easier if you omit the browning in a skillet. Browning and simmering can be done in a Dutch oven. Spoon the batter on top and pop it into the oven to bake, then bring directly to the table. The meat pie tastes the same. It just doesn't look quite so pretty.

Minestrone

2 medium carrots
2 white turnips
3 or 4 medium zucchini
3 stalks celery
3 medium ripe tomatoes, peeled,
    or 2 cups peeled canned
    tomatoes
3 or 4 leaves romaine lettuce or
    escarole

1 large mealy potato
½ teaspoon oregano
1½ tablespoons finely chopped
    fresh basil, or 1 teaspoon
    dried
1 pound beef short ribs
salt and fresly ground pepper to
    taste
about ½ cup freshly grated
    Parmesan cheese

Bring 8 cups of water to a boil in a large kettle. Cube the carrots, turnips, and zucchini. Slice the celery into small chunks. Chop the tomatoes and shred the romaine. Peel the potato and leave it whole. Add all the vegetables, the oregano, and the basil to the boiling water, dropping the potato in last.

The short ribs should be as lean as possible. But, as by nature they are never really lean, remove a bit of the fat, then add the ribs to the vegetables.

Simmer minestrone covered for 4 hours at least, then allow it to rest. Simmer for another 4 to 5 hours the next day. This is not always feasible, so let it simmer for as long as possible.

After 3 or 4 hours the bones will have separated from the meat and can easily be removed. Do so. And, as the minestrone continues to cook, the meat will practically disintegrate. It should. If there are some rather large chunks left, tear them apart with the help of 2 forks.

At this point the potato should also have more or less disintegrated. Without removing it from the kettle, mash it with a potato masher.

Just before you are ready to serve, taste the soup and add salt and pepper according to your taste. Salt very lightly because the vegetables contain salt and so does Parmesan cheese.

If you serve the minestrone from a tureen or in individual dishes, sprinkle with the Parmesan, or pass the cheese separately in a small bowl at the table.

On very cold winter nights I have been known to add 1 cup of dry red wine at the end. Keep in mind that if you have any minestrone left over it will be even better the next day.

Serves 6 as a meal-in-one or 8 as a first course.

■

Hamburger Patties with Bitters

1 pound lean ground beef   *2 tablespoons Angostura bitters*

Sirloin or eye round would be best for this dish. Place the meat in a bowl and add the bitters. Mix very well. You will have to use your hands; a spoon simply can't do the job.

Divide the meat into patties and either place in a preheated broiler or pan broil in a skillet, as you wish. Don't use any other seasonings. Angostura does it all.

Serves 4 to 5

NOTE: This use of bitters has very recently been brought to my attention. It is the result of the ever-growing realization that sodium isn't good for us and that we should limit our intake of it as much as possible. It seems that bitters contain very little sodium. I have given the quantity that suits my taste but you may, of course, use more or less. The flavor is surprisingly subtle.

Eggplant and Noodle Casserole

2 small eggplants
salt
about ⅓ cup olive oil
½ pound noodles, white or
  spinach

1 pound very lean ground beef
freshly ground pepper to taste
2 tablespoons unsalted butter
1 cup feta cheese, crumbled

Slice the eggplants fairly thin but don't peel them. Sprinkle with salt and let stand for 10 minutes or so. Pat dry with paper towels.

Heat the oil in a large skillet over medium-high heat and fry the eggplant slices a few at a time. Don't crowd them in the skillet. When they are golden, remove them to paper towels.

Bring at least 3 quarts of water to a strong boil in a large saucepan. The more water pasta has to cook in the better. Stir in 2 tablespoons of salt and add the noodles. Cook a few minutes less than it tells you on the package.

Preheat the oven to 350°.

While the pasta is cooking, add the meat to the hot oil in which you fried the eggplant. Stir with a wooden spoon and allow to brown over high heat. Add pepper but no salt.

Grease a deep oven-proof baking dish with a little of the butter.

Drain the noodles and toss with 1 teaspoon butter.

Mix the meat with the feta cheese and layer about ½ of the mixture in the casserole. Add layers of ⅓ of the noodles and ½ of the eggplant. Continue layering until all the ingredients are used up. The top layer should be noodles dotted with the remaining butter.

Bake for about 30 minutes, or until the top is golden brown.

Serves 6

NOTE: I advise against salting the meat because the feta is quite salty.

This dish may be prepared well ahead of time and placed in the oven when your guests arrive.

It is unlikely that you will have any left over but if you do, you'll enjoy it reheated the next day.

■

Beef and Ham Casserole

3 tablespoons unsalted butter
1 small onion, chopped fine
2 pounds lean ground beef
½ cup coarsely chopped cooked
  ham

2 tablespoons soy sauce
  (optional)
1 large egg
½ cup chopped peeled tomatoes

Preheat the oven to 350°.

Melt the butter in a skillet and sauté the onion until it is limp and translucent, but not brown. Add the beef and the ham. Sauté until the beef has lost its raw look. Add the soy sauce. Remove from the heat and add the egg. Mix until it is thoroughly amalgamated.

Fill an 8-inch casserole with the mixture and cover with the chopped tomatoes.

Back, uncovered for about 30 minutes. Serve with steamed rice or, for a change, with steamed buckwheat or barley.

Serves 5 to 6

NOTE: I suggest the ham because it adds a slightly spicy flavor. But if you have leftovers of other meats or chicken, they may be used instead.

If you use soy sauce, you won't need either salt or pepper. If you don't like the taste of soy, you will want to use other seasoning: salt, pepper, and maybe a little oregano.

Veal with Tuna Sauce

1 piece of veal (2 pounds), cut
   from the leg
2 stalks celery
1 small onion
1 carrot
boiling water
3 bay leaves
½ cup dry white wine
pinch of salt

1 can (7 ounces) tuna packed in
   oil
8 anchovy filets
3 tablespoons capers
½ cup mayonnaise, preferably
   homemade (page 194)
juice of ½ lemon
1 lemon, sliced thin

The veal should be of the finest quality possible and should not be rolled. It should look like a filet of beef, only smaller and pinker. Wrap it tightly in cheesecloth and tie securely at both ends, leaving rather long loops on either side.

Place the celery, onion, and carrot in a large, deep saucepan and pour in boiling water to cover the vegetables by a depth of about 1-inch. Add the bay leaves, wine, and salt and place the saucepan over high heat. When the water returns to a boil, lower the meat into it, allowing the loops to hang over the sides for easy removing. There should be enough water to just cover the meat and vegetables.

When the water returns once more to a boil, lower the heat and simmer gently for about 1 hour, or until the veal is tender. Let it cool in the broth.

Place the tuna (with oil), anchovies, and 1 spoonful of the capers in a blender or food processor and mix until blended. Add the mayonnaise and mix until creamy. Add the lemon juice and enough of the broth to thin the sauce to the consistency of very heavy cream.

When the meat is cool enough to handle, lift it from the broth, remove the cheesecloth, and place the meat on a cutting board. It should be quite cold so that it will be easier to slice. Don't refrigerate it, though; it might dry out.

Slice the meat as thin as possible and arrange the slices on a serving platter, overlapping slightly. If you are not going to serve it immediately, pour a little of the tuna sauce over it, just enough to keep it moist. Cover with plastic wrap as tightly as possible. Place the rest of the sauce in a bowl and cover it as tightly as possible to prevent discoloration. The moistened meat and the sauce may be refrigerated up to 24 hours.

When you are ready to serve, coat the meat with the rest of the sauce, making sure all slices are covered. Sprinkle with the remaining capers and garnish with the lemon slices. Serve at room temperature.

Serves 4 to 6

NOTE: This is certainly not a recipe for those on a tight budget. Veal is frightfully expensive, and you don't get much mileage out of it because it shrinks in cooking. If you want to cheat and use breast of turkey instead of veal, be very careful when covering the meat with the sauce; the tiniest piece of snow-white meat that remains exposed is a giveaway. But once the turkey has soaked in the tuna sauce, no one will know the difference.

Veal Scaloppine with Sage Butter

1 pound veal from center of leg,
  cut into 8 slices
3 tablespoons unsalted butter
2 fresh sage leaves or ½
  teaspoon dried

coarse salt
freshly ground white pepper
lemon wedges

Use only veal of the best quality. Place the meat between 2 sheets of plastic wrap or put in a plastic bag (see note). Pound with a short metal mallet until flattened to less than ¼ inch. With a very sharp knife, make small cuts at intervals in the edges of the meat. This will prevent them from curling while cooking.

Melt the butter in a large skillet and add the sage immediately. Don't allow the butter to brown. Over high heat, add the meat, a slice at a time. The meat must not be crowded in the pan; it would get soggy.

Brown the meat quickly on one side. Turn, using tongs so you don't pierce the meat, and brown on the other side. As soon as they are cooked, place the slices on a warm platter, overlapping a little. Sprinkle lightly with salt and a little freshly ground white pepper. Pour the sage butter over the slices. Place lemon wedges around the meat; some people like to squeeze a little lemon over each bite.

Serves 4

NOTE: This is the basic preparation of this delicious and luxurious meat. There are innumerable variations. You might want to add chopped capers to the butter, in which case you won't need salt, or decorate the slices with small curls of anchovy filets. Most green vegetables go well with veal scaloppine, as will mashed or boiled potatoes, or rice.

Placing the slices of meat in a plastic bag is a new trick I have just learned. The meat can't slide out, as often happens when you use 2 sheets of wax paper or plastic wrap.

Veal Birds with Black-Olive Stuffing

2 pounds lean veal, sliced thin
 (as for scaloppine)
1 slice (about ¼ pound) calves
 liver
4 anchovy filets
½ teaspoon juniper berries

3 tablespoons butter
½ cup olive oil
1 cup chicken or beef broth
1 cup pitted and chopped Greek
 or Italian oil-cured black
 olives

Beat the veal slices until quite thin (see note on page 224). They shouldn't be larger than 4 by 4 inches; if they are too large, cut them to size.

Chop the liver and the anchovies. Crush the juniper berries. Mix liver, anchovies, and juniper berries with the butter to make the stuffing.

Place the veal slices on a flat board and put about a tablespoon of the stuffing in the center of each slice. Roll the veal and secure with toothpicks.

Heat the oil in a skillet large enough for the rolls to cook in one layer without crowding. When oil is hot, add meat and cook over medium heat for about 15 minutes, turning every now and then and adding a couple of spoonfuls of broth whenever the meat seems to be getting too dry. Add the olives and cook a couple of minutes longer. Serve hot, with either rice or boiled potatoes.

Serves 8

NOTE: This dish may easily be prepared ahead and reheated.

Veal Stew with Fresh Peas

2 pounds boneless lean veal for
   stew, cubed
1 tablespoon unsalted butter
1 tablespoon oil
½ cup chicken or beef broth

½ cup chopped ham (optional)
1 cup shelled, fresh young peas
½ cup dry white wine
salt and pepper to taste

Cut off any bone or stringy tendons from the veal, but don't remove every bit of gristle and fat; they add flavor and thicken the broth. Pat the meat dry.

Heat the butter and oil in a large skillet. Add the meat over high heat and, using tongs so you don't pierce the meat, turn the pieces rapidly to brown them on all sides.

Lower the heat to medium and add the broth, ham, and peas, stirring with a wooden spoon. Bring to a boil, reduce heat, and cover the pan. Simmer very gently for 10 minutes and add the wine. Simmer for an additional 10 minutes, stirring occasionally. Add the salt and pepper. You may add a little more broth or wine or a mixture of both if necessary to maintain liquid in the pan. The stew should be moist, but not soupy.

Serves 6

Sautéed Veal Kidneys

6 small veal kidneys
juice of 1 lemon
3 tablespoons oil
½ cup dry vermouth

dash of Worcestershire sauce
  (optional)
freshly ground black pepper to
  taste
1 tablespoon finely chopped
  parsley

Most variety meats are an acquired taste, and I acquired a taste for veal kidneys very early in life. I am not equally bullish on lamb or beef.

Peel their thin outer membrane and cut the kidneys in half lengthwise. Remove the white core with a sharp knife. Pour the lemon juice over the kidneys and let stand for a few minutes. Slice about ¼ inch thick and pat dry.

Heat the oil in a large skillet over medium-high heat. Add the slices, taking care not to crowd them, and sauté very quickly just until no blood is visible. Add the vermouth, turn the heat to low, cover the skillet, and cook for about 10 minutes. Kidneys toughen if they are cooked too long.

If you are going to add the Worcestershire, and I recommend it, don't use too much pepper. This is the moment to add both.

Sprinkle with the parsley and serve immediately.

Serves 6 to 8

NOTE: You can stretch veal kidneys by adding sliced mushrooms to them. The procedure remains the same. Serve with rice cooked al dente.

Lamb and Eggplant Casserole

2 medium eggplants (the long
   and narrow kind), unpeeled
about 3 tablespoons oil
1 small onion

1 pound lean ground lamb
1 teaspoon curry powder
salt to taste
1 cup canned, peeled tomatoes

Cut 1 eggplant into lengthwise slices about ¼ inch thick. Heat half the oil in a skillet and fry the eggplant slices, a few at a time, until they are translucent. Add oil as needed. Place the slices on paper towels to absorb excess oil.

Chop the other eggplant and the onion and mix well with the lamb. Add the curry powder and salt and mix well.

Preheat the oven to 350°.

Butter a casserole and cover the bottom with eggplant slices, reserving a few for later use. Fill the casserole with the lamb mixture and cover with the remaining eggplant slices. Chop the tomatoes coarse and pour over the eggplant slices.

Cover and bake for 30 minutes. Uncover and test the meat. If it has the desired doneness, bake uncovered for another 10 minutes, or until the top is slightly crisp.

Serves 4 to 5

Broiled Lamb Patties

1 pound lean ground lamb
1 small onion
6 mint leaves, minced

salt and pepper to taste
sprigs of mint or parsley for
  garnish
mint sauce or English mustard

Place the meat in a mixing bowl and break up with a fork.

Peel the onion and grate it on an old-fashioned grater, using the small holes. Hold the grater over the mixing bowl so the grated onion and its juice drip in.

Add the mint leaves, salt, and pepper and mix well with your hands. (That's the part I don't like because the meat gets under my nails and is hard to get out. But there simply is no other way to distribute the onion and mint evenly throughout the meat.)

Shape the meat into 4 patties and refrigerate them briefly.

Preheat the broiler.

Broil the patties about 6 inches from the heat for 6 minutes on each side. The patties will be medium rare.

Place the patties on a heated platter and decorate with sprigs of mint or parsley. Serve with mint sauce or English mustard.

Serves 4

NOTE: Spring is the season for lamb and, if you want to cook a leg or a rack of lamb, that is when you should do so. For patties, lamb of any season can be used. If your meat is very lean, you might be better off sautéing the patties in a tablespoon of butter. The broiler might dry them out.

Bean Curd (Tofu) with Brussels Sprouts

½ pound Brussels sprouts
  (preferably fresh)
4 tablespoons olive oil
1 pound soft bean curd (tofu)
1 teaspoon coarse salt

1 teaspoon freshly ground black
  pepper
¼ cup freshly grated Parmesan
  cheese

Wash and trim the Brussels sprouts. If you are using frozen sprouts, don't defrost them.

Heat 2 tablespoons olive oil in a large skillet, add the sprouts (fresh or frozen), and, stirring with a wooden spoon, sauté them over high heat until they are nicely coated. If you use frozen sprouts, cover and cook over medium heat until they are thoroughly defrosted and begin to lose their raw look.

Add the rest of the oil. Cut the bean curd into 1-inch slices. The best way to do this is slice it with a slotted spatula while it is still in the water in which it lives and carefully lift it out with the same spatula. Dry on paper towel.(If you have a better system don't hesitate to use it.) After the Brussels sprouts have cooked about 5 minutes, raise the heat under the skillet, move the sprouts to one side, and add the tofu slices to the hot oil. Don't disturb them for a couple of minutes; they will form a crust. Sprinkle them liberally with salt and pepper (tofu is bland), then turn them gently. They should be golden on both top and bottom, and no matter how gently you treat them, they might crumble a little. It does not matter. When both the tofu and the sprouts are done (about 10 to 12 minutes in all), sprinkle them liberally with Parmesan cheese and serve.

Serves 4 to 6

NOTE: Tofu might be an acquired taste. It didn't take me long to get to like it. I had encountered it frequently in Chinese dishes and felt that it could probably be used in Western cuisine as well. I seem not to be the only one to think so because, whereas tofu used to be found only in oriental stores, it is now widely available, often sold in 1-pound squares in water. Buy it only where it is kept under refrigeration, and cook it for at least 2 minutes. Tofu is very perishable. Keep it in fresh water in the refrigerator. Properly stored, tofu will stay fresh for 3 to 4 days.

This recipe is very far removed from Chinese uses of tofu. Like most of my recipes, it has an Italian touch. Instead of Brussels sprouts, you could use broccoli or cauliflower rosettes.

Bean Curd (Tofu) with Eggplant

4 small oval-shaped eggplants
   (Italian eggplants)
6 tablespoons olive oil
1 teaspoon coarse salt

1 pound soft bean curd (tofu)
1 teaspoon freshly ground black
   pepper
2 tablespoons chopped basil

Cut the eggplants into lengthwise slices no more than ¼ inch thick. The thinner, the better.

Heat 3 tablespoons of the olive oil in a large skillet over medium heat. Pat the eggplant slices dry with a paper towel and add them to the skillet without permitting the sides to overlap. When they start to brown and become translucent, turn them with a spatula and allow to brown on the other side. Have a paper towel spread out next to the skillet and transfer the slices to it as they brown, replacing them with raw ones. Add more oil as it is needed. Eggplant absorbs a lot of oil; the paper towel will absorb the surplus. Sprinkle slices with some of the salt while they are hot.

Slice the tofu as described in the preceding recipe. Heat the remaining oil in the same skillet and add the tofu slices. Sprinkle with remaining salt and add the pepper. Sprinkle the basil over them. When the tofu slices are golden, return the eggplant slices to the skillet just long enough to reheat them, and serve.

Serves 4 to 6

NOTE: Both the tofu and the eggplant may be prepared ahead of time. Keep the eggplant on the towel until ready to serve and add briefly to the tofu over high heat. Eggplant has great personality and needs no Parmesan. However, if you feel like splurging, you might add a little. It only improves the flavor.

ACCOMPANIMENTS

 hat would you serve with it?" is the question I am most frequently asked when I write or speak about recipes.

What indeed?

It seems to me that there are only a few basic rules: If the main course has a sauce or a gravy, don't serve an accompaniment that has another one. If you want to serve a salad, use a separate plate.

I have mentioned earlier my feelings about serving noodles as a side dish, but I want to repeat that, instead of the eternal rice or the ubiquitous potatoes, buttered barley or buckwheat are nice alternatives. Familiar vegetables, prepared in an unfamiliar way, are also a great addition to one's repertoire. For example, serve grated zucchini or try green beans with tomatoes.

Carrot Soufflé

1½ pounds carrots
3 large eggs at room
   temperature
⅓ cup milk

1 tablespoon all-purpose flour
2 tablespoons bourbon
salt and pepper to taste

Bring to a boil enough water to cover the carrots. Add the carrots and cook until tender.

When the carrots are done, place them under cold running water until they are cool enough to handle. Remove the skin; it will come off very easily. Cut each carrot into 3 or 4 pieces and place in a food processor or food mill. If you use a food processor, turn the motor on and off a few times so that the carrots are coarsely puréed. Transfer to a mixing bowl.

Preheat the oven to 400°.

Separate the eggs and add the yolks, 1 at a time, to the carrots, mixing thoroughly and being careful that each egg is amalgamated before adding the next. In another bowl, mix the flour with the milk, stirring until there are no lumps. Add the bourbon, stir to blend well, and add the mixture to the carrots. Season with salt and pepper.

Beat the egg whites until stiff and fold them into the carrot mixture. Pour the batter gently into a buttered 6-inch soufflé dish and place it in the center of the oven. Bake for 25 to 30 minutes, opening the oven door only after the soufflé has baked at least 25 minutes. If you like a dry soufflé, leave it in the oven a few minutes longer.

Serves 4 to 6

NOTE: This soufflé will not rise as high as most. The carrot mixture is heavier than the usual soufflé base. But this is a beautiful and delicious dish; even people who normally hate carrots like it.

Spicy Carrot Casserole

8 medium carrots, cooked
    under-done and cut into
    slices about ⅓ inch thick
2 tablespoons grated onion
2 tablespoons freshly grated
    horseradish

½ cup mayonnaise, preferably
    homemade (page 194)
salt and pepper to taste
2 tablespoons unsalted butter
½ cup bread crumbs
dash of paprika

Preheat the oven to 350°.

Place the carrot slices in a baking dish. Mix the onion, horseradish, mayonnaise, salt, and pepper and pour over the carrots.

Melt the butter in a skillet and add the bread crumbs. Stir until the butter is absorbed but don't brown the crumbs.

Cover the carrots with the buttered bread crumbs, place the baking dish in the oven, and bake for 15 to 20 minutes, or until the bread crumbs look crisp. Sprinkle paprika over the top. Serve hot.

Serves 4

Purée of Knob Celery

3 or 4 knob celery (celeriac)
½ lemon (optional)
2 cups broth, preferably beef

freshly ground pepper to taste
2 tablespoons unsalted butter

When buying knob celery look for firm, medium- to large-size heads. Very large knobs may be old and woody. Wash them and remove the roots. Peel the knobs, using a very sharp paring knife. Dig out any dark spots. Rub the knobs with lemon to avoid discoloration. (This is only a cosmetic gesture and is not imperative.) Bring the broth to a boil, then cut the knobs into chunks and add to the broth. Boil for about 10 minutes, or until they are translucent and easily pierced with a fork. Drain and let cool.

If you have a food processor, place a few pieces at a time in the bowl and run the sharp blade, turning on and off, until you have a smooth purée. If it looks a little runny because some broth is left in it, transfer the purée to a saucepan and cook briefly until it thickens to the consistency of mashed potatoes. Add the pepper and stir. I omit salt in the recipe because the broth is usually salty enough. Add the butter, stir, and serve very hot.

Serves 4

NOTE: This is one of my favorite vegetable recipes. It may also be prepared with Jerusalem artichokes. If neither is available, white turnips will do—but add 2 tablespoons of freshly grated Parmesan cheese along with the butter. The dish can be prepared ahead of time and reheated at the last moment.

Baked Fennel (Finocchio)

1 large bulb fennel
2 tablespoons butter

⅓ cup freshly grated Parmesan cheese
freshly grated white pepper to taste

Preheat the oven to 350°.

Cut the long stems from the fennel, cutting close to the bulb; discard stems. The outer layer, which should be discarded, will come off by itself. Cut the bulb into slices ¼ inch thick. Rinse slices. Bring a saucepan of water to a boil and add fennel. Cook for about 5 minutes, or until it has lost its raw look. Drain.

Butter a rectangular baking dish and arrange the fennel slices neatly on the bottom; they should overlap a little. Dot fennel with most of the butter, then sprinkle the Parmesan over and dot with remaining butter. Sprinkle with pepper. Place the baking dish in the oven and bake for about 20 minutes or until the top is golden.

Serves 4

NOTE: I find that people stay away from fennel because they don't know what to do with it. This is my favorite recipe, but fennel is also delicious raw as addition to a green salad or by itself with a cheese dip. When buying fennel, be sure you get a male bulb. The male bulb is round and the stems stick straight up. The female is rather flat and the stems stick out sideways. When you cut the females, they are less firm. As for the pepper, I suggest using white only because it looks better on the white fennel.

Green Beans with Ham

1 pound fresh tender green
   beans
¼ pound cooked ham
2 ripe medium tomatoes
1 small onion

2 tablespoons unsalted butter
2 tablespoons olive oil
2 tablespoons finely chopped
   parsley

Wash the beans and snap the ends off. Chop the ham into coarse dice. Peel and chop the tomatoes. Slice the onion very thin.

Melt the butter in a skillet and add the oil. Add the onion and sauté until it is translucent but not brown. Add the ham, stir in the tomatoes, and then the green beans. Cover and let simmer for about 20 minutes, or longer if you like your vegetables well cooked. Uncover every now and then to make sure that all the liquid from the tomatoes hasn't evaporated. If the beans seem too dry, add a little water. Just before removing the skillet from the heat, add the chopped parsley. Serve very hot as an accompaniment to a veal roast or boiled chicken.

Serves 4

NOTE: If you increase the quantity of ham, this dish may be served as a main course for a simple luncheon. The recipe is a very good way to use up leftover ham.

If the green beans in the market seem a little old and limp, try the long beans available in most oriental markets. They are about 10 to 12 inches long and very slender. Cut them in 3- to 4-inch pieces and cook them as you would our regular green beans.

Mushrooms with Lemon and Eggs

1 pound fresh mushrooms
1 tablespoon unsalted butter
3 tablespoons olive oil

juice of 1 medium lemon
salt to taste
2 large eggs

Remove the sandy bottoms from the mushrooms and separate the stems from the caps. Wipe the caps with a damp cloth. Remove the sandy part of the stems. Slice both the caps and the stems.

Heat the butter and oil in a large skillet. (You don't want to crowd the mushrooms.) As soon as the mixture is hot, add the mushrooms and sprinkle the lemon juice over them. Add a little salt, stir, and cover the skillet with a lid. Cook for 6 to 8 minutes, stirring once or twice. When the mushrooms are done they should be white.

Beat the eggs in a small bowl. Turn off the heat under the mushrooms but don't remove them from the burner. Pour the eggs over them and allow to set.

Serves 4

Sesame Baked Potatoes

6 unblemished Idaho potatoes
6 tablespoons unsalted butter

6 teaspoons sesame seeds
salt and freshly ground pepper
to taste

Scrub the potatoes and pierce with a fork in a couple of places. You may bake them in a preheated 450° oven for 1 hour, or, at the same time as a roast, at 350° for about 1 hour and 30 minutes. The baking time will depend on the size of the potatoes.

If you bake your potatoes in aluminum foil, unwrap them partially when they are done, leaving foil around the lower part. Make a deep incision in the top. Scoop out some of the potato and, with a small spoon, make a deep well without breaking the potato. Place 2 tablespoons of butter in the well and, with the spoon, press it into the pulp.

Sprinkle the sesame seeds into the well and mix them with the hot buttered potato, taking care not to break the skin. Add salt and pepper. Replace the pulp you scooped out and mash it into the buttered part.

If you don't plan to serve them immediately, close the foil over the potatoes and place them on a hot tray. If you don't use foil (I use a baking spike), place the buttered potatoes in a lukewarm oven with the heat turned off.

Serves 6

NOTE: This also works well as a first course at a very informal dinner.

You never know when you will come across a good new idea. I was traveling on a train recently when an elegant man with a briefcase in one hand and a small shopping bag in the other sat down across from me. He placed the briefcase across his knees, opened the shopping bag, removed a Styrofoam box, and placed it on the briefcase. He opened the box and removed a plastic knife and fork. "This is like a picnic," he said. "Want a bite?" I refused smilingly (to his relief, I think).

He so obviously enjoyed what he was eating that I couldn't help asking what it was. The box it came in prevented me from seeing what was a baked potato, filled with butter and sesame seeds, as described in this recipe. He had bought it from a stand in Grand Central Station.

This seemed like such a good idea that I couldn't wait to get home to try it. It was indeed delicious, probably even more so since it had been standing for awhile before he started eating it. I have since tried it also with curry powder—I like it, but then I have a weakness for curry powder. Try it; the amount of curry powder you put in depends, of course, on your personal taste.

Cold Dilled Potatoes

6 large mealy potatoes
⅓ cup very fine olive oil
2 egg yolks
½ cup finely chopped fresh dill

juice of ½ large lemon
freshly ground pepper to taste
1 small onion (optional)
½ cup crumbled feta cheese

Peel the potatoes and place them in a saucepan with just enough cold water to cover them. Bring to a boil and cook the potatoes over high heat. By the time they are done the water should be absorbed. If the water is evaporating too fast, lower the heat and simmer, stirring with a wooden spoon so the potatoes don't stick to the bottom.

When all the water is gone and the potatoes are tender, mash them with a potato masher while the potatoes are still hot. Add the oil and then the egg yolks, 1 at a time, mixing well until the oil and eggs are absorbed. Add the dill, which must be fresh; if none is available, use Italian parsley, though the result will be different. Add the lemon juice and mix. Taste the mixture: if you like a slightly tart taste add a little additional lemon juice. Add freshly ground pepper.

If you are devoted to the taste of onion, grate the onion very fine and add.

Place the mixture in a shallow bowl and refrigerate for at least 2 hours. Before serving, sprinkle the feta cheese over it. Serve cold on a buffet or as a side dish as you would serve a salad.

Serves 6 to 8

NOTE: I first encountered this dish in a Turkish restaurant and was too proud to ask what was in it. My companion however asked and was told that recipes weren't given. I have since made it several times, and this recipe duplicates that restaurant's version exactly.

Sautéed Spinach with Parmesan

2 cups cooked spinach, tightly
   packed
3 tablespoons oil
3 tablespoons freshly grated
   Parmesan cheese

salt to taste (optional)
pinch of freshly grated nutmeg
1 hard-cooked egg white,
   chopped fine (optional)

Make sure all the water has been squeezed out of the spinach. Heat the oil in a skillet and add the spinach. Spread it out in the pan with a fork, then stir so that it is evenly coated. Sauté for several minutes. It is alright if some of the leaves get a little crisp. Add salt, if you wish, and the nutmeg and Parmesan, and mix.

Transfer the spinach to a serving dish. You may wish to sprinkle the chopped egg white over the spinach. The egg is just a decoration and not a must, but it is a good way to use leftover egg whites.

Serves 4 to 6

NOTE: I am a dangerous spinach eater, and I could easily eat this whole recipe as a main course, although for some people this quantity could easily serve more than 6.

Parsley Purée Villa Mozart

4 bunches Italian parsley
    (about 1 pound)
boiling water
ice cubes
5 tablespoons butter

1 shallot, chopped
5 tablespoons heavy cream
½ teaspoon freshly ground
    white pepper
salt to taste

Wash the parsley thoroughly. The slightest trace of sand can ruin this delicate recipe. Remove and discard the stems. Place the leaves in boiling, lightly salted water to cover and boil for exactly 3 minutes. While they are boiling prepare a large bowl of ice. Drain the parsley leaves in a large colander and *immediately* cover them with ice cubes. That will prevent the green from turning dark. As soon as the parsley is cool enough to handle squeeze all the water out with your hands. There should be 2 cups, very tightly packed. Place a little at a time in your food processor and, using the sharp blade, purée the first batch. Continue until all the parsley is puréed. Place the parsley in a mixing bowl.

Melt half the butter in a skillet, add the shallot, and sauté until it is translucent but not brown. Spoon the shallot and butter into the parsley and return the mixture to the food processor. Still using the sharp blade run the motor for a few seconds, pushing down what clings to the sides, and process again. Add the cream and run the motor for a few seconds to amalgamate. Melt the remaining butter and add to the purée. Add the white pepper, run the motor, and then taste the purée; at this point you might want to add a little salt. Personally, I feel it doesn't need any. Parsley is quite salty.

Scrape the contents of the food processor into a saucepan, reheat briefly, and serve.

Serves 6

NOTE: You might consider this recipe too much trouble for just a side dish but it is delicious, most unusual, and may be made ahead of time. It can also be served the next day. To reheat it you might add a few drops of cream.

I learned the preparation of this distinctive dish in the kitchen of the Villa Mozart in Merano, working with chef-owner Andrea Hellrigl, one of the great, innovative chefs of Europe.

Zucchini Stew with Fresh Basil

4 large zucchini squash
3 or 4 large very ripe tomatoes
    or 4 to 5 cups peeled canned
    tomatoes

⅓ cup olive oil
½ cup coarsely chopped basil
    leaves, tightly packed
salt and pepper to taste

Here is a use for any overgrown zucchini squash you may discover lurking under the vine leaves in your garden or find on sale.

Cut the squash into lengthwise quarters and core them as you would an apple. The center is too spongy to be edible, so discard it. Cube the remaining shell. Your needn't peel it unless the skin is tough.

Place the cubes in a large saucepan over high heat for 30 seconds, stirring with a wooden spoon to prevent sticking. This will cause some of their water to evaporate. Lower the heat to medium and stir in the oil. Simmer about 5 minutes, stirring frequently.

Remove any blemishes from the tomatoes, peel them, remove the seeds, and squeeze out the liquid. If you use canned tomatoes, pour off most of their liquid.

Add the tomatoes, salt, and pepper and mix well. The tomatoes should practically disintegrate. If too much liquid appears on the surface, raise the heat a little; the liquid will evaporate quicker.

Add the chopped basil and mix well. When the basil is completely wilted, the stew should be ready. Serve hot.

Serves 4 to 6

NOTE: This stew may be served on spaghetti or tagliatelle as a tomato sauce. Sprinkle a couple of tablespoons of freshly grated Parmesan cheese on top.

Onion or peppers may be added to the stew, but I love the taste of fresh basil so much that I don't want to overpower it with other strong flavors.

Grated Zucchini Sauté

6 firm medium zucchini
1 tablespoon salt
⅓ cup olive oil
freshly ground pepper to taste

½ teaspoon freshly grated
  nutmeg
2 tablespoons fresh parsley

Wash the zucchini and trim the ends. Remove all blemishes (better if they don't have any to begin with). Shred the zucchini coarse. This can be done using the large holes on an old-fashioned grater or the shredding disk of a food processor.

Place the grated zucchini in a bowl and sprinkle with salt. Don't worry about oversalting them. Let stand for at least 30 minutes.

Scoop up some of the zucchini with your hands and squeeze. This will eliminate a lot of water, and the salt will go with it.

Heat the oil in a large skillet, add the zucchini, and sauté over high heat for 1 minute to evaporate any remaining liquid. Lower the heat to medium and sauté for a few minutes. Stir in the pepper and nutmeg. Just before serving, sprinkle with parsley.

Serves 4 to 6

NOTE: I have served this dish to a number of culinary experts. Not one of them has been able to identify the vegetable, the most frequent guesses being broccoli or eggplant. (Sometimes I wonder why I go through the trouble of grating the zucchini. Why don't I just serve them broccoli? Because I love this dish, that's why!)

If you feel like splurging, add a couple of tablespoons of freshly grated Parmesan cheese to the zucchini just before adding the parsley. It will add to the cost of this otherwise inexpensive dish, but if you use just any old grated cheese, you do the zucchini no favor.

Fried Zucchini Blossoms

12 fresh zucchini blossoms	1 large egg
½ cup all-purpose flour	oil for frying (preferably olive oil)
½ cup bread crumbs	coarse salt

Wash the blossoms under running water and dry them very gently with paper towels.

Spread the flour on a flat surface and the bread crumbs on another. Beat the egg in a small bowl. Heat the oil in a skillet. With your fingers, dredge the blossoms lightly in the flour, taking care not to bruise them. With a fork, dip the blossoms in the egg, making sure they are well coated. Then dip them in the bread crumbs and drop them in the hot oil, a few at a time, so as not to crowd them.

Gently turn blossoms with a spatula. When they are golden, remove them from the oil and drain on a paper towel. Sprinkle with salt and serve hot.

Serves 4

NOTE: This will raise eyebrows. Who usually serves zucchini blossoms? I shall never forget my husband's look when I served them and told him what they were. Now I am lucky if he leaves me a couple.

The problem is that the blossoms must not be wilted. If you are lucky enough to have a garden, you can pick the blossoms just before dinner. They can occasionally be found in specialty produce markets—you might ask your greengrocer to keep them for you. Or ask your neighbors for them. Most home gardeners grow zucchini but ignore the blossoms.

Strawberry-Raspberry Mold, page 250

DESSERTS

Desserts are a challenge. Some guests like them very sweet, some not so sweet, and no one likes them fattening.

So we compromise. Simple fruit can be the answer for the "not-fattening" crowd. But is it really satisfying? You can add all sorts of cheeses, but there goes the "not-fattening" bit.

So we might as well give in: desserts are fattening. There are, however, degrees of sinfulness and in the following pages you will find some recipes that won't do you permanent bodily harm.

Strawberry-Raspberry Mold

1 package (10 ounces) frozen
    strawberries
1 package (10 ounces) frozen
    raspberries
1 package (6 ounces) strawberry
    gelatin

1 package (6 ounces) raspberry
    gelatin
2 cups heavy cream
1 cup fresh strawberries or
    raspberries (optional)

Defrost both packages of frozen berries, retaining the liquid. Place both in a blender or a food processor and purée. Place in a large saucepan and heat but don't bring to a boil. Remove from heat and immediately add both packages of gelatin. Stir until completely dissolved. Pour the mixture into a large bowl and let it cool, but don't allow it to set.

Shake the container of cream before opening it. If the cream stands on a shelf for any length or time part of the fat will separate on top. By shaking the container you mix it with the rest of the cream.

Beat 1 cup of the cream until very firm and gently but thoroughly fold it into the cooled fruit mixture. Fill an 8-cup ring mold (or whatever shape mold appeals to you) with the mixture and refrigerate. After a couple of hours it will unmold without any difficulty.

Whip the remaining cream until firm and spoon it over the mold. If berries are in season, you might fill the center of the mold with them. You could also omit the second cup of cream and use only berries for decoration. This will make for a less rich dessert.

Serves 6

NOTE: I had eaten this delicious dessert in the home of an Italian ambassador to the UN, and had thoroughly enjoyed it, as had all other guests. One day I sneaked into the kitchen and asked the cook for the recipe. I could hardly believe that it would be so simple. She told me that her boss frequently had guests at very short notice. She always kept the ingredients for this dessert handy, and she always made it with overwhelming results.

Three-Colored Cream

1 quart milk
4 large eggs
8 tablespoons granulated sugar
2½ tablespoons sifted flour
2 tablespoons cornstarch

peel of ½ lemon
1 tablespoon vanilla extract
1 tablespoon sifted cocoa
1 tablespoon instant coffee
  powder

Pour the milk into a large, heavy saucepan. Over very low heat, add gradually the remaining ingredients with the exception of the cocoa and the coffee. Mix vigorously with a wire whisk until the cream thickens and comes almost to a boil; don't allow it to boil.

Remove the lemon peel. Divide the cream into 3 even parts, then add the coffee to one part and the cocoa to the second; leave the third part as it is. In a glass or crystal bowl, make layers of the 3 creams, separating the coffee and cocoa layers with a layer of the plain. If you prefer, fill 6 individual glass cups. Whatever you use should definitely be transparent. Chill and serve.

Serves 6

Chocolate Mousse

6 ounces quality semisweet
   chocolate
⅓ cup strong hot coffee
1 tablespoon granulated sugar
2 tablespoons unsalted butter

4 large eggs, separated, and
   whites at room temperature
3 tablespoons amaretto liqueur
   or crème de menthe
small pinch of salt

Break the chocolate into small pieces, place in the bowl of a food processor, and add the coffee, which should be very hot. Process, using the steel blade, turning the motor on and off, until the chocolate is dissolved. Add the sugar and run the motor a few seconds longer. Add the butter and process until well amalgamated. Add the egg yolks, 1 at a time, running the motor briefly in between. Add the liqueur and process.

In a bowl beat the egg whites until very stiff. Add a small pinch of salt for best results. Pour the chocolate mixture into a serving bowl and gently fold in the whites. Chill well before serving.

Serves 8

NOTE: If you wish, you can decorate the surface with little curlicues of whipped cream. Personally, I find it rich enough without it. Brandy may be substituted for the amaretto or crème de menthe.

Pear Mousse

4 ripe Bartlett pears
1 envelope unflavored gelatin
½ cup warm water

3 large eggs at room
   temperature
⅓ cup granulated sugar

Peel and core the pears. Cut them into chunks and place them in the bowl of a food processor. Using the sharp steel blade, process until the pears are puréed.

Sprinkle the gelatin over warm water to soften.

Place the pear purée in a saucepan and add the gelatin. Stir and heat briefly until the gelatin is totally dissolved. Let cool, then transfer to a serving bowl.

Separate the eggs and beat the yolks with the sugar until they are pale yellow. Gently mix in the pears.

Beat the whites until stiff peaks form. Add the whites a little at a time and fold into the pear-yolk mixture, using a rubber spatula. Chill.

Serves 4

Pineapple Mousse

1 can (20 ounces) pineapple
   chunks
1 teaspoon vanilla extract
3 tablespoons rum or kirsch
juice of ½ lemon
1 tablespoon confectioners'
   sugar, according to taste

5 large eggs, separated at room
   temperature
1 teaspoon all-purpose flour
12 candied violets

Drain the pineapple and reserve the syrup for some other use. (If you like sweet pineapple juice, drink it while you are preparing the mousse!) Place the chunks in a blender and whirl at high speed. Transfer to a bowl, add the vanilla and the rum or other spirits (vodka will do), and stir. Add the lemon juice, stir, and chill.

Add the sugar to the egg yolks and beat well. Add the flour and beat until smooth. Add to the pineapple.

Beat the egg whites until quite stiff. If the peaks are not stiff enough, add a small pinch of sugar.

Add the whites to the pineapple mixture, folding them in very gently but thoroughly. Transfer mixture to a serving bowl or into 6 individual bowls and refrigerate for at least 2 to 3 hours. Before serving, place 2 violets in the center of each small bowl or make a circle of them around the rim of the large bowl.

Serves 6

NOTE: This is a very light dessert, suitable for the end of a hefty meal. If you can't find candied violets, a sprinkling of shredded coconut will do, but the effect is less elegant.

For a heavier mousse you may dissolve an envelope of unflavored gelatin in ½ cup warm water and stir it into the pineapple. It will add substance to the mousse. However, without gelatin the mousse may be prepared a day ahead; made with gelatin, a day-old mousse would get rubbery.

Pineapple chunks are usually packed in heavy syrup. Personally I find them sweet enough to add almost no sugar or very little. But that is a question of personal taste. I always keep a can of pineapple handy in case of sudden guests. As for the other ingredients, you probably are never without them anyway.

Don't be dismayed if you find that the top is airy while some of the pineapple mixture settles at the bottom of the dish and seems a little soupy. When you start eating them the top and the bottom get mixed together and are delicious.

Watermelon Mousse

1 envelope unflavored gelatin
1 medium watermelon
½ cup granulated sugar

8 teaspoons liqueur (kirsch,
    brandy, framboise, or poire)
1 cup strawberries, blueberries,
    or raspberries

Soften the gelatin in a little hot water and dissolve.

Cut the watermelon in half lengthwise, then into slices. Remove the rind and all the seeds. Cube the flesh and place in a blender with the sugar. If you have a food processor, place the pieces of watermelon first in the processor and then in the blender: you will get a smoother purée. Measure purée; you should have 2 cups. Add the dissolved gelatin. Fill 8 serving cups with the melon and refrigerate. When ready to serve, pour 1 teaspoon of liqueur over each cup and garnish with berries.

Serves 8

NOTE: The watermelon purée may be frozen, either in a plastic container or in an ice-cube tray. When you are ready to use it, defrost and place briefly back in the blender, then add the gelatin, liqueur, and berries.

If you need only half the watermelon for this dessert, you can make a fruit boat with the shell: scoop the flesh out with a melon baller and place them in a bowl. Add 1 banana, cut into rounds, 1 pear, cubed and sprinkled with lemon juice to avoid discoloration, and whatever berries are in season. Toss the fruits gently with sugar and liqueur to taste and put them in the watermelon shell. Refrigerate and, at the moment of serving, place the fruit boat on a platter or in a large oval bowl, add a few sprigs of mint and serve with 2 large serving spoons.

Oranges with Mint

4 large juicy navel oranges
about 1 tablespoon granulated
   sugar

about 2 tablespoons crème de
   menthe
1 tablespoon coarsely chopped
   mint leaves

Peel the oranges, carefully removing the pith, and cut oranges into rather thin slices. Arrange them on 4 dessert plates or in a bowl.

Sprinkle sugar and crème de menthe to taste over the oranges and let stand for at least 30 minutes, preferably longer (even overnight). Refrigerate them if you like.

Just before serving, sprinkle the oranges with the mint leaves.

Serves 4

NOTE: We have all served oranges flavored with one liqueur or another. Grand Marnier seems to be the most popular. Crème de menthe, particularly with the addition of mint leaves, is a totally different experience. I also like to use rum; its flavor combines well with mint.

When chopping the mint, keep the pieces large. If chopped too fine, they tend to look too dark.

Fruit Salad with Cream

2 juicy navel oranges, peeled
and cut into chunks
2 bananas, sliced
2 apples (McIntosh or similar)
peeled, cored, and cut into
chunks
2 ripe pears, peeled, cored, and
cut into chunks

1 cup fresh pineapple chunks
(canned may be
substituted)
1 cup heavy cream (see note)
4 tablespoons rum (light or
dark)
1 tablespoon confectioners'
sugar (optional)
2 tablespoons pine nuts

Prepare the fruit over a bowl to catch all the juices. Place the cut fruit in a porcelain or glass bowl; never use metal or wood. If you use canned pineapple, drain it well and reserve the juice.

Mix the cream, rum, and reserved fruit juices and add the sugar, if desired. Mix well so the sugar dissolves. Pour over the fruit mixture, scatter the pine nuts over the top, and serve chilled.

Serves 6

NOTE: There are 2 kinds of heavy cream on the market: one is pasteurized, the other is ultra-pasteurized. Stay away from the latter. It doesn't whip well and leaves an unpleasant aftertaste.

Sugared Figs

12 fresh ripe figs
½ cup confectioners' sugar

6 tablespoons water
2 tablespoons kirsch

Choose the figs carefully. They should be ripe and soft. I prefer the green figs to the purple because they usually have a thinner skin.

Preheat the oven to 400°.

Place the sugar in a shallow bowl. Rinse the figs under running water, 1 at a time. While they are wet, dip them in the sugar to cover them all over. Arrange the figs in a well-buttered baking dish just large enough to hold them upright. Mix the water with the kirsch and gently pour the liquid around the figs. Place the dish in the center of the oven and bake for about 10 minutes, or until the coating has caramelized. Serve at room temperature.

Serves 4 to 6

NOTE: This is the easiest dessert but not the cheapest. In the East I would serve 2 figs per person. In the West, where figs are more affordable, you would probably serve 3 per person. If the tips of the figs are not sticky, they can be eaten with the hands.

Pears with Meringue Topping

6 ripe pears (Bosc or other firm
    variety)
1 cup dry white wine
1 teaspoon vanilla extract
½ cup granulated sugar

1 tablespoon brandy or cognac
5 egg whites, at room
    temperature
pinch of salt (optional)

Peel and core the pears and slice them. You should have about 8 slices per pear. The pears should not be overripe, nor should they be of the very soft variety, juicy though they be.

Place the slices in a large skillet where they won't be heaped on top of one another. Add the wine, the vanilla, and half the sugar. Bring to a gentle boil. The pears will give off a lot of liquid; simmer until the liquid is almost gone. If the pears are particularly juicy and the liquid tends to make them too mushy, drain off some of the liquid.

Preheat the oven to 275°.

Place the pears in a shallow baking dish—good-looking enough to come to the table and large enough for the pears not to be in a heap. Pour the brandy over them.

Beat the egg whites, adding the remaining sugar after you have started beating them. If you wish, add a pinch of salt. Beat until the whites are very stiff.

Cover the pears with the beaten egg whites, swirling on tall peaks. Place the dish in the preheated oven and bake until the whites are set and the peaks are golden, about 15 to 20 minutes. Serve lukewarm or cold.

Serves 6

Spiced Pears with Whipped Cream

6 firm ripe Bosc pears
⅓ cup granulated sugar
4 whole cloves

1 cup heavy cream
1 teaspoon ground cinnamon

Peel, halve, and core the pears. Place them, cut side down, in a large skillet, arranging them so their sides don't touch. Add water to barely cover. Sprinkle with sugar. Add the cloves, making sure that they don't touch the pears (cloves leave dark spots on fruit). Simmer gently for about 30 minutes, or until the pears are tender when tested with a fork.

Very gently, remove pears and place them in a shallow bowl, adding a little of the poaching liquid but discarding the cloves.

Beat the cream until firm. Distribute it all around the pears and in the center of the bowl. The pears should not be completely covered. Sprinkle the cinnamon over the cream. Serve cold or at room temperature.

Serves 6

NOTE: If you like your desserts very sweet, add sugar to taste to the cream when you have almost finished whipping it. Don't add it in the beginning: it will moisten the cream and prevent peaks from forming.

Dried Apricots and Peaches with Cream

½ pound dried peaches
½ pound dried apricots
½ cup granulated sugar

3 tablespoons rum or kirsch
1 small piece vanilla bean,
*   about 1 inch (optional)*
1 cup heavy cream

Soak the peaches and apricots in lukewarm water for about 1 hour, or until they are fairly soft. Exact time for soaking can't be given because some dried fruit is softer than others. Drain.

Bring 2 cups of water to a boil and add the fruit, sugar, (and vanilla bean, if desired). Allow to simmer, uncovered, for about 1 hour and 30 minutes. The fruit should be quite soft when tested with a fork. There should be very little liquid left, barely enough to cover the bottom of the saucepan. If there is more, pour off a little. (Drink it, it's good.) Remove the vanilla bean, let cool, and add the rum or kirsch.

Place the fruit in a serving bowl. Whip the cream until quite firm and cover the fruit completely with it. If you wish to make the dish more spectacular, pulverize 5 Italian macaroons (called amaretti) and sprinkle them over the top.

Serves 8 to 10

NOTE: This dish may also be served warm, but I have an awful recollection of a dinner I gave one summer in the country. It was a huge party, and I had a helper in the kitchen who assured me he knew a dessert that was out of this world. I had already prepared appetizers, first course, main course, vegetables... I gladly turned the dessert over to him. This, with the addition of prunes, was the dessert, and he brought it to the table steaming hot. The day had been in the high nineties and had barely cooled off. I haven't seen him since.

Eva's Marshmallow Dessert

1 pint heavy cream
1 tablespoon confectioners'
sugar
1½ cups miniature
marshmallows

1 cup assorted nuts (no
peanuts), chopped
1 teaspoon vanilla extract
1 teaspoon almond extract
1 tablespoon bourbon

In a large mixing bowl, start beating the cream. When it is still soft, add the sugar and continue beating until stiff peaks form.

Place the cream in a serving bowl and add the other ingredients 1 at a time, mixing gently. Add the bourbon at the very end or shortly before serving.

Scoop out individual portions.

Serves 4

NOTE: This recipe was given to me by a Texan relative of my husband. I managed not to look skeptical, but I was; and as I can't resist a recipe, no matter how improbable, I tried it. It is delicious, though very rich. After I served it the first time, however, I modified it a little. Instead of chopped nuts, I pulverized 5 Italian macaroons and folded them into the mixture. Then I added 1 more macaroon (meaning 2 halves, since they come as 2 half-rounds in a paper wrapper) which I only crumbled and scattered over the surface. It was a different flavor, and was even more popular with my guests.

Ricotta Pudding with Chocolate

1 pound whole milk ricotta
⅓ cup granulated sugar
3 hard-cooked egg yolks
grated rind of ½ lemon
2 tablespoons light rum

3 tablespoons grated semisweet
    chocolate
3 egg whites
boiling water

Empty the container of ricotta onto a paper towel and place another towel on top. Let stand for at least 10 minutes. The towels will absorb the excess liquid.

Preheat the oven to 350°.

Place the ricotta in a bowl and stir well with a wooden spoon. Add the sugar and stir. Strain the yolks through a fine sieve and add to the ricotta. Add the lemon rind, rum, and chocolate and stir to amalgamate well. Beat the egg whites until very stiff and fold them carefully into the ricotta mixture.

Butter a 1-quart mold or soufflé dish, spoon the ricotta mixture into it, and place the mold in a shallow baking pan. Place in the oven and pour in enough boiling water to come halfway up the sides of the mold. Bake for about 1 hour.

Serves 6 to 8

NOTE: Ideally this pudding should be served warm. If it is allowed to cool it will fall a little, but it will still taste good. I prefer it plain, but it may be served with a light chocolate sauce or a strawberry sauce.

Fruited Farina

3 cups milk
1½ cups farina
½ cup granulated sugar
1 teaspoon pure vanilla extract
   or 1-inch piece of vanilla
   bean
4 tablespoons unsalted butter
½ teaspoon salt

½ teaspoon finely grated lemon
   zest
2 whole eggs
1 egg yolk
1 tablespoon all-purpose flour
about 2 tablespoons
   confectioners' sugar
1 cup fresh berries according to
   season (optional)

Preheat the oven to 350°.

Bring milk to a slow boil and gradually add the farina, stirring constantly to avoid lumping or sticking. Stir in the granulated sugar, add the vanilla extract or vanilla bean, and continue stirring. Cook for about 10 minutes, then remove from the heat. Add 3 tablespoons of the butter, salt, and lemon zest. Allow to cool; then add the eggs, 1 at a time, and the yolk. Mix well until totally amalgamated.

If a vanilla bean has been used, remove it at this point.

Butter an 8-inch soufflé dish making sure all sides are well coated, and dust with the flour. Pour the mixture into the mold and place in the center of the oven. Bake for 1 hour. Remove it from the oven and let stand for a few minutes, then unmold it onto a platter and sprinkle with confectioners' sugar.

If berries are in season, scatter them over the top of the mold and all around it. If not, dilute the contents of a jar of good strawberry jam with a little water and a teaspoon of kirsch. Serve the warm sauce on the side.

Serves 6 to 8

NOTE: If unmolding unsettles you (don't be ashamed, it affects the best of us), the mold may be served in the dish in which it was baked. Serve the confectioners' sugar and the berries separately for people to help themselves.

Crêpes à la Crème

2 cups milk
¾ cup sifted flour
2 large eggs plus 2 egg yolks
⅓ cup plus 1 teaspoon
granulated sugar
2 tablespoons cornstarch

pinch of salt
2 teaspoons butter,
approximately
1 tablespoon confectioners'
sugar
½ cup Grand Marnier or other
orange liqueur, warmed

Pour 1 cup of milk into a bowl and add the flour a little at a time. For best results, pour it through a sieve as you add it. Using a wire whisk, beat the flour and milk until completely amalgamated. Add the whole eggs, one at a time, and continue beating until the mixture is smooth. Add the 1 teaspoon of sugar and beat a little longer. Let the mixture stand for 1 hour.

While the batter is resting, prepare the custard. Heat the remaining milk in a saucepan but don't allow it to boil. Combine the yolks, remaining sugar, salt, and cornstarch in a bowl. Beat with a whisk until totally blended. Add the hot milk in a thin stream, beating constantly. When the milk is incorporated, transfer the mixture to the saucepan where you heated the milk. Over low heat, continue beating with the whisk until the mixture thickens; don't allow it to boil. Let the mixture cool—it should have the consistency of a thick mayonnaise. Set aside briefly.

When batter has rested, heat an 8-inch skillet over medium heat. As soon as warm, place about ½ teaspoon butter in the center and move the skillet from side to side and up and down until bottom is evenly coated. Dip an average ladle into the batter until half filled. Pour the batter into the center of the skillet and immediately lift the skillet off the heat, rotating it so that the batter covers the whole surface. Place the skillet back on the burner and cook the crêpe until golden on the underside. Shake the skillet now and then to make sure batter doesn't stick to bottom. After about 1 minute, lift an edge to see if done. Place a plate on top of skillet and, with a rapid turn of your hand, drop the crêpe onto the place, cooked side up.

Using the corner of a paper towel, pick up a tiny amount of butter and rub it over the surface of the skillet. Slide the crêpe back into it, browned side up. When other side is done, slide onto a platter and continue cooking other crêpes. You should have about 12 crêpes.

Place crêpe on a flat board and put about 1 teaspoon of custard in the center. Fold like a bundle, then transfer—folded side down—to a heatproof platter. Continue with remaining crêpes. Sprinkle on the confectioners' sugar and bring to the table, carrying the Grand Marnier in the other hand. Pour the liqueur generously over and ignite. Allow flames to die, then serve 3 crêpes per person.

Serves 4

NOTE: The crêpes can be prepared ahead of time. Just place a sheet of wax paper between each and stack for refrigerator or freezer.

During a recent visit to Paris I was taken to a charming restaurant. There were 6 of us and we all ordered these crêpes. One lady was in a bad mood and as soon as she had tasted her crêpe she shrieked, "Far too much alcohol." As if Grand Marnier were just alcohol! She transferred the crêpes to another plate while I happily lapped up the liqueur.

Sherbet with Pernod and Saffron Villa Mozart
(For owners of ice cream makers only!)

2¼ cups water
½ cup sugar (granulated or
   confectioners')
juice of 5 lemons

pinch of pure saffron
3 ounces Pernod
2 egg whites

Bring the water to a boil and add half the sugar. Simmer until a light syrup forms. Add the lemon juice, the saffron, and the Pernod. Let cool, then pour the mixture into the ice cream maker, and start freezing it, according to manufacturer's directions.

Beat the egg whites until very firm, then slowly add the remaining sugar. When the sugar has been amalgamated place the bowl over a pan of boiling water and continue beating until the egg whites are really solid.

When the Pernod-saffron mixture has begun to freeze add the egg whites, incorporating them gently, and continue to freeze until the sherbet is solid.

Serves 6

NOTE: This sherbet is served in small glasses, not as a dessert but in the middle of the meal to cleanse the palate. We are frequently served so-called "palate cleansers" that are too sweet to clear our taste buds. This one really does what it is supposed to do. It is one of the inventions of Andrea Hellrigl, the master chef of the Villa Mozart in Merano, in the very north of Italy near the Austrian border.

Andrea, born on the Swiss-Italian border, started cooking at the age of fifteen. Today he is one of the great cooks of Europe, attracting devoted followers from many countries. He doesn't advertise and seeks no publicity. Cooking is his profession and his hobby, and the Villa Mozart, an architectural gem, his pride and joy.

If you have the original saffron that looks like a miniature plant with tiny twigs, one of those twigs is the perfect quantity of saffron for the sherbet. If you use the powder form, a hefty pinch will do. The important thing is that it be real saffron with no artificial anything.

Andrea di Merano makes a variation of this sherbet with Campari, the Italian aperitif. The procedure is the same, but you use dry white wine instead of water and double the sugar as Campari is very bitter.

■

Ice Cream with Peach Sauce

1 cup peach preserves
2 tablespoons lemon juice
3 tablespoons cognac

1 pint ice cream, preferably vanilla or coffee
1 tablespoon shredded coconut (optional)

Place the peach preserves in a small saucepan and heat but don't bring to a boil. Add the lemon juice and stir. Add the cognac and stir again. Let cool.

Scoop the ice cream into individual bowls and spoon the sauce over it.

Decorate the ice cream with shredded coconut if you wish, or top with a couple of candied violets. If you use coffee ice cream, use candied mimosa.

Serves 4 to 5

CONVERSION TABLES

The following are conversion tables and other information applicable to those converting the recipes in this book for use in other English-speaking countries. The cup and spoon measures given in this book are U.S. Customary; use these tables when working with British Imperial or Metric kitchen utensils.

LIQUID MEASURES

The old Imperial pint is larger than the U.S. pint; therefore note the following when measuring the liquid ingredients.

U.S.
1 cup = 8 fluid ounces
½ cup = 4 fluid ounces
1 tablespoon = ¾ fluid ounce

Imperial
1 cup = 10 fluid ounces
½ cup = 5 fluid ounces
1 tablespoon = 1 fluid ounce

U.S. Measure	Metric	Imperial*
1 quart	946 ml	1½ + pints
1 pint	473 ml	¾ + pint
1 cup	236 ml	− ½ pint
1 tablespoon	15 ml	−1 tablespoon
1 teaspoon	5 ml	−1 teaspoon

*Note that exact quantities cannot always be given. Differences are more crucial when dealing with larger quantities. For teaspoon and tablespoon measures, simply use scant quantities, or for more accurate conversions rely upon metric measures.

WEIGHT AND VOLUME MEASURES

U.S. cooking procedures usually measure certain items by volume, although in the Metric or Imperial systems they are measured by weight. Here are some approximate equivalents for basic items.*

	U.S. Customary	**Metric**	**Imperial**
Apples (peeled and sliced)	*3 cups*	*500 g*	*1 pound*
Beans, dried (raw)	*2½ cups*	*450 g*	*1 pound*
Butter	*1 cup*	*250 g*	*8 ounces*
	½ cup	*125 g*	*4 ounces*
	¼ cup	*62 g*	*2 ounces*
	1 tablespoon	*15 g*	*½ ounce*
Cheese (grated)	*½ cup*	*60 g*	*2 ounces*
Cornstarch	*1 teaspoon*	*10 g*	*⅓ ounce*
Cream of Tartar	*1 teaspoon*	*3-4 g*	*⅛ ounce*
Flour, all-purpose (sifted)	*1 cup*	*128 g*	*4¼ ounces*
	½ cup	*60 g*	*2⅛ ounces*
	¼ cup	*32 g*	*1 ounce*
Herbs, fresh	*¼ cup whole*	*15 g*	*½ ounce*
	2 tablespoons chopped	*7 g*	*¼ ounce*
Mushrooms, fresh (chopped)	*4 cups*	*300 g*	*10 ounces*
Nut meats	*1 cup*	*112 g*	*4 ounces*
Peas, fresh (shelled)	*1 cup*	*450 g*	*1 pound*
Potatoes (mashed)	*2 cups*	*450 g*	*1 pound*
Raisins (or Sultanas)	*¾ cup*	*125 g*	*4 ounces*
Rice	*1 cup (raw)*	*225 g*	*8 ounces*
	3 cups (cooked)	*225 g*	*8 ounces*
Spinach, fresh (cooked)	*½ cup*	*285 g*	*10 ounces*
Sugar:	*1 cup*	*240 g*	*8 ounces*
granulated	*½ cup*	*120 g*	*4 ounces*
	¼ cup	*60 g*	*2 ounces*
	1 tablespoon	*15 g*	*½ ounce*

*So as to avoid awkward measurements, some conversions are not exact.

	U.S. Customary	Metric	Imperial
Confectioners'	1 cup	140 g	5 ounces
	½ cup	70 g	3 ounces
	¼ cup	35 g	1 + ounce
	1 tablespoon	10 g	¼ ounce
Brown	1 cup	160 g	5⅓ ounces
	½ cup	80 g	2⅔ ounces
	¼ cup	40 g	1⅓ ounces
	1 tablespoon	10 g	⅓ ounce
Tomatoes, fresh (peeled, seeded, juiced)	1½ cups	450 g	1 pound
Zucchini	3½ cups (sliced)	450 g	1 pound
	2 cups (grated)	450 g	1 pound

OVEN TEMPERATURES

Gas Mark	¼	2	4	6	8
Fahrenheit	225	300	350	400	450
Celsius	107	150	178	205	233

PHOTOGRAPH CREDITS
AND ACCESSORIES

We are grateful for the assistance of the following sources in supplying accessories for the color photographs included in this book.

Photo 1: *Buckwheat Noodles with Olive Sauce:* plate "Pincio Red" from R. Ginori; Parmesan server also from R. Ginori. Underplate from Fitz & Floyd.

Photo 2: *Cheese Topped with Polenta:* polenta machine from Todaro Bros.

Photo 3: *Shrimps with Peppers and Feta:* copper pot and ladle from R. Ginori, by Nazzucata.

Photo 4: *Swordfish with Peas:* platter, salt & pepper "Palerma Red" from R. Ginori.

Photo 5: *Chicken with Mushrooms and Tomatoes:* platter "Ventadour" by Bernard Limoges, from Cardel, Ltd. Salt & pepper "Astral," from Cardel, Ltd. Candlestick "Imperial" crystal, from Cardel, Ltd.

Photo 6: *Minestrone:* tureen from R. Ginori.

Photo 8: *Strawberry-Raspberry Mold:* plate "Imperatrice" by Haviland Limoges, from Cardel, Ltd.

Matthew Klein, photographer
Susan E. Johnson, stylist
Andrea Swenson, food preparation

RECIPE INDEX*

*__Boldface__ page numbers refer to suggested seasonal menus in which the recipes may be used.

GENERAL INDEX

decanters, wine, 34
decorations, limited money for, 25–27,
    112–113
desserts:
    for limited help parties, 53, 66
    for limited time parties, 21, 24, 33
dining rooms, 40
dishes. *See* plates; serving dishes
dress, host's/hostess', 10–11
drinks. *See* liquor; wine

eggs:
    at picnics, 83
    stored at room temperature, 2
    stuffed, chilling of, 3
entertaining, reasons for, 59–60, 73,
    87, 89–90
entrance halls, as dining rooms, 42
entrances, lighting of, 9

fish:
    cold, for buffet, 17
    poached, 17, 19
    purchase of, 21–22
    removal of spine, 19
    served on platter, 28
flatware:
    matched versus unmatched, 27
    for picnics, 81
    for poolside parties, 85
    salad forks for main courses, 41
    on set table, 50, 64
flowers:
    arrangement of, 5
    expense of, 25
    keeping fresh, 4–5
folding tables, 42–43, 52
fontina, 109
frittata, 46
fruit:
    cut and marinated, 21
    as dessert, 33, 66, 68, 86
    grapes, 86
    purchased fresh, 2
    stored at room temperature, 2

glasses:
    breaking of, 45
    matched versus unmatched, 27
    for picnics, 81
    plastic, 85
    for poolside parties, 85
    set out, for after-theater parties, 22
    storage, 37
    water, 41
    wine, 27, 41, 45
guests:
    boring, 51, 73–74, 77
    clumsy, 45, 102–103
    coats of, 42, 70
    difficult, 97–104
    late, 5–6
    unexpected, 94–95

hampers, picnic, 83
help, limited, for parties, 47–70
herbal teas, 23
hostesses:
    "great," 71–74
    lack of, 63–70
    shy, 74–77
hosts, lack of, 54–61
hot trays, 4, 52

ice:
    for chilling food, 3–4
    at poolside parties, 84–85
    purchase of, 3
ice buckets, 80
invitations:
    date, 6–8
    by mail, 6–7
    R.S.V.P., 7–8
    style, 8
    by telephone, 6–7
    telephone confirmation, 6
    time, 5–6
Italian cheeses, 17, 29, 34, 46, 82,
    108–110
Italian cooking, 31
Italian wines, 34, 69, 111